WHO KEEPS THE SCORE
ON THE LONDON STAGES?

Contemporary Theatre Studies
A series of books edited by Franc Chamberlain, Nene University College
Northampton, UK

Please see the back of this book for other titles in the Contemporary Theatre
Studies series

WHO KEEPS THE SCORE ON THE LONDON STAGES?

Kalina Stefanova
*National Academy for Theatre and Film Arts,
Sofia, Bulgaria*

harwood academic publishers
Australia • Canada • France • Germany • India
Japan • Luxembourg • Malaysia • The Netherlands
Russia • Singapore • Switzerland

Amsteldijk 166
1st Floor
1079 LH Amsterdam
The Netherlands

British Library Cataloguing in Publication Data
Who Keeps the score on the London stages? – (Contemporary
    theatre studies; v. 36)
    1. Theatre critics – Interviews   2. Dramatic criticism – Great
    Britain
    I. Stefanova, Kalina
    792'.015

ISBN 90-5755-116-0

CONTENTS

INTRODUCTION TO THE SERIES

Contemporary Theatre Studies is a book series of special interest to everyone involved in theatre. It consists of monographs on influential figures, studies of movements and ideas in theatre, as well as primary material consisting of theatre-related documents, performing editions of plays in English, and English translations of plays from various vital theatre traditions worldwide.

Franc Chamberlain

LIST OF INTERVIEWEES

LONDON DRAMA CRITICS

Paul Allen	BBC
Kate Bassett	*The Daily Telegraph*
Michael Billington	*The Guardian*
James Christopher	*The Times* and freelance
Michael Coveney	*The Daily Mail*
Nick Curtis	*The Evening Standard*
Nicholas de Jongh	*The Evening Standard*
Jane Edwards	*Time Out*
John Elsom	Honorary President of the International Association of Theatre Critics
Lyn Gardner	*The Guardian*
Robert Gore-Langton	*The Sunday Express*
John Gross	*The Sunday Telegraph*
Bill Hagerty	*The News of the World*
Peter Hepple	*The Stage*
Ian Herbert	*Theatre Record*
Robert Hewison	*The Sunday Times*
Jeremy Kingston	*The Times*
Alastair Macaulay	*The Financial Times*
Sheridan Morley	*The Spectator*
David Nathan	*The Jewish Chronicle*
Benedict Nightingale	*The Times*
John Peter	*The Sunday Times*
Ian Shuttleworth	*The Financial Times*
Charles Spencer	*The Daily Telegraph*
Jack Tinker	former critic of *The Daily Mail*
Irving Wardle	former critic of *The Times* and *The Independent on Sunday*
Matt Wolf	London theatre critic for *Variety* and Associated Press

PLAYWRIGHTS AND DIRECTORS

Sir Alan Ayckbourn	playwright/director, Stephen Joseph Theatre

Steven Berkoff   playwright/director/actor
Howard Davies   director
David Edgar   playwright
Sir Richard Eyre   director
David Farr   director
Sir Peter Hall   director
Jonathan Kent   artistic director, Almeida Theatre
Nicolas Kent   artistic director, Tricycle Theatre
Sam Mendes   artistic director, Donmar Warehouse
Katie Mitchell   director, The Royal Shakespeare Company
Adrian Noble   artistic director, The Royal Shakespeare
                                  Company
Trevor Nunn   artistic director, The Royal National Theatre
Max Stafford-Clark   artistic director, Out of Joint Theatre
Arnold Wesker   playwright

PRODUCERS

Thelma Holt
Sir Cameron Mackintosh
Michael Morris
Tom Morris
Peter Wilkins

PRESS-AGENTS AND A PUBLISHER

Martin Coveney
Nick Hern   publisher, Nick Hern Books
Sue Hyman
Sharon Kean
Sue Rolfe
Joy Sapieka

ACKNOWLEDGEMENTS

Is there anyone whom I should not thank? That is the question as I start writing these acknowledgements.

I wish to thank many, many people and one institution.

The institution is The British Council which gave me an Award as a Visiting Scholar at City University, London – a grant that enabled me to spend five months in London, this Mecca of theatre.

I acknowledge the people in chronological order of their appearance in my life. First, my dear friends Professor John Elsom, my artistic adviser at the University, and Ian Herbert – the two people who personally introduced me to the London theatre critics, theatre-makers and press-agents. They helped me until the completion of my work on this book – John with his encouragement and insights, and Ian forwarding my mail from London to Bulgaria. Then David Stokes, previously head of The British Council in Bulgaria; Dessislava Stoicheva, Dora Kamarska and Aglika Markova from The British Council in Bulgaria; Susan Widdington who gave me the key to her house in the fifth minute of our first meeting – to be her housekeeper while she was in the US; Andrew and Svetla Vladovi who did the same for me afterwards; and later Elizabeth Gorla and then David Lea, thus helping me to survive in London and fulfil my task; Mira Martin and the rest of the Bulgarian Section of the BBC World Service; all my interviewees, who were so perceptive and informative in their interviews, and so helpful to me in the course of my research; Ljubov Shtilianova who exercised endless patience in transcribing the 55 cassettes of interviews; and Michael Coveney who was kind enough to help me decipher some of his colleagues' handwritten corrections for my benefit, and some of my English for the readers.

I am really proud that I may now count many of these people among my friends.

PROLOGUE:

THE BRITISH DIMENSION OF THE AMERICAN DREAM

In one respect, the American Dream comes true not in America but in London: when it comes to theatre criticism. Or so I discovered talking to the major New York theatre critics and theatre makers in the course of a two-year research in New York in the beginning of the '90s.*

I had gone there in search of my ideal blueprint for theatre criticism. I had read an article about the then ubiquitous Frank Rich and, since in Bulgaria theatre critics had never wielded any influence whatsoever, let alone power, I had set out on a journey to discover the mechanisms which made American theatre criticism so important.

I did discover them, but I also discovered that some of them were paradoxes, or even shortcomings, rather than virtues. In brief, the ideal didn't turn out to be quite so ideal.

Maybe, I thought, the ideal is a kind of mixture of the European model of theatre criticism and the American one at their best? Almost unanimously the New York theatre critics and theatre-makers were pointing to London. "Theatre criticism over there is something of the kind," they said.

So I set out on a new journey to discover if that was true. In taking a snap-shot picture of the London theatre criticism scene I was helped by the major London critics and theatre-makers who were kind enough to give me interviews on this subject.**

---

* published in the book *Who Calls the Shots on the New York Stages?* Harwood Academic Publishers, 1994
** I conducted the interviews in 1996 and they were subsequently revised and updated by my interviewees in 1997 and 1998.

Part I
In Their Capacity As An Ideal:
Enter The London Theatre Critics

1

ROADS TO PERFECTION: 27 WAYS TO BECOME A THEATRE CRITIC IN LONDON

Paul Allen
Kate Bassett
Michael Billington
James Christopher
Michael Coveney
Nick Curtis
Nicholas de Jongh
Jane Edwards
John Elsom
Lyn Gardner
Robert Gore-Langton
John Gross
Bill Hagerty
Peter Hepple

Ian Herbert
Robert Hewison
Jeremy Kingston
Alastair Macaulay
Sheridan Morley
David Nathan
Benedict Nightingale
John Peter
Ian Shuttleworth
Charles Spencer
Jack Tinker
Irving Wardle
Matt Wolf

They answer the questions:

– *When, how, and why did you make up your mind to become a theatre critic? Was that a continuation of a family tradition? How has your career evolved through the years?*

PAUL ALLEN:

I wanted to be a journalist and I wanted to specialize in the arts. Of course, the arts were not seen as very important and, in any case, first you have to learn typing and shorthand, the law and the rules, so I spent two years being an apprentice. After I had proved I was a serious journalist by doing other things, I started specializing in theatre. Then the time came when I also wanted to write plays, so I gave up my job and became a freelance. I did some reviewing for *The Guardian* and *The New Statesman* and various other papers, and I was writing plays at the same time. It was almost casual that I became involved in radio. I had done a little bit of local radio. In Sheffield in North England where I lived, there was somebody who had been reviewing for *Kaleidoscope* and who moved away to another part of the country. So I asked whether I could review for them. They tried me out on one review and then almost immediately they said, "Do you want to present the programme?" The first one I did was somewhere around 1980. Then I would spend half of my time writing and the other half – on the radio. But then the time came when they said, "We have to concentrate on a handful of presenters and have them work with us. Are you prepared to do it every week?" I said, "Yes." ... I have enjoyed the job very much but it has stopped me writing. I can review for *The Guardian* any time I want to but I just don't have the time. And I don't believe in one person reviewing one thing twice. When you present a radio programme, you can steer very clearly the way the reviewer goes. Even if it becomes an argument, you can still have your say.

KATE BASSETT:

In my early twenties I was working both in the theatre and as a freelance arts journalist and had not absolutely decided which path to take. In the theatre I worked, mostly as an assistant director, for the Gate, Hampstead and The Royal Court. My last post was at The National Theatre Studio — as 'Young Director On Attachment'. In terms of arts journalism, I was writing for various publications: a few reviews in *The Guardian, Time Out*, some features in *The Spectator, The TLS*.

Just as the post at the Studio ended, Ian Shuttleworth – the theatre editor of *City Limits* magazine – asked me to be his deputy. Then, when *City Limits* folded, the arts editor of *The Times* offered me a job as their third theatre critic. I was very lucky. That was a great job to get at 25. At that point, I knew I couldn't have a foot in both camps anymore. On the continent, people seem both to work in the arts and write as arts journalists. But it's very difficult to be frank and objective if you mingle with the people whose work you then appraise.

Because I studied English – which involves literary criticism – and because I'd worked in the theatre, I think I felt drawn to and confident about being a critic. Thinking further back, as a child I remember being really thrilled – skipping in the Aldwych after my parents took me to see, it must have been

Love's Labours Lost. I got a real kick out of seeing theatre as a child. I don't skip about much in the Aldwych anymore, but really brilliant theatre still thrills me.

It wasn't a family tradition. My family, on both sides, worked in teaching – with a lay preacher and a Cornish smuggler sometime way back. My father is a civil engineer and university lecturer. My mother was an infant school teacher. She encouraged me to love the arts. My brothers work in computing and medicine though, thinking about it, my brother (the doctor) used to do lots of theatre lighting and was member of the theatre society at the college I also went to. He encouraged me unstintingly when I wanted to join in. So maybe there's a mini-tradition there. Also my grandfather wrote a terrible stage adaptation of a Chekhov short story when I was about sixteen, sent me a copy and asked my opinion. My opinion did not go down well. He wrote me a very sniffy letter back. Still, maybe he started me off all the same. How has my career evolved through the years? Well, I've gone from being the third critic at *The Times* to the second critic at *The Telegraph*. I'm not paid 20 pounds per review anymore either – which was *City Limits'* rate – that's if you ever got the pay cheque. I get to see better shows, generally, now. I'm slightly wary of the idea of pure evolution. There's a theory that critics have eight years of decent reviews in them, which is an alarming thought. My end is nigh, if the theory's right.

MICHAEL BILLINGTON:

My devotion to theatre criticism has something to do with Stratford-upon-Avon. I was born eight miles from there, and what used to be called the Shakespeare Memorial Theatre – now the RST – was a kind of Mecca for me. I remember being taken there at the age of eight to see *Troilus and Cressida*. Later I became addicted to that theatre and by the age of 16–17 I'd seen the bulk of Shakespeare's work performed by actors of the highest calibre like Laurence Olivier, John Gielgud, Michael Redgrave, Peggy Ashcroft. I'd also seen modern plays, pantomimes, and the music hall in Birmingham and Coventry. This wide variety of theatre was, of course, a major influence. But the job of the critic is determined to some extent by temperament as well. I've always been a watcher. I've felt I'd rather be a commentator than a doer. I suppose it has something to do with a sort of reclusive and bookish temperament. This is why I prefer to stay in the room called *Prospero's Cell* when I'm at the Shakespeare Hotel in Stratford-upon-Avon.

I went to university in Oxford and studied English. Strangely enough, the way the English exam system works is in a sense a journalistic training. You spend three years studying literature and then your degree is determined by a week of two-hour exams in which you have to write everything you know about a subject. I was very involved in the theatre in

Oxford: I wrote for student newspapers, I acted and directed. So when I left there were only two things I was keen to do: theatre criticism and directing.

I went to journalism in Liverpool, unsuccessfully. Then I went into the theatre for two years in Lincoln hoping to run a repertory company. It was very useful but I decided I wasn't born to be a part of the theatre. So I came to London, in 1964, and spent a long time just looking for work. The turning point came in the spring of 1965, when a friend came to tea and suggested that I write a letter to *The Times*. By then I had already a stack of reviews. *The Times'* arts editor liked them and set me off to see a production of Shaw's *Saint Joan* in Bristol. Thank God, from that moment on he just kept commissioning me – week in, week out. So it was a combination of determination, of wanting desperately to be a theatre critic – I thought that was what I was chosen to be – and good luck. *The Times* editor, John Lawrence, was a patron not just to me but to a number of other critics, like John Peter and Irving Wardle. He was magnificent in giving us encouragement, work, and commitment. For the next six years I kept running around theatres, films, and TV, doing interviews and writing articles. This was my training as a critic.

Now I get letters from people who say, "I want to be a drama critic. How can I become one?" The answer is: There is no formula. But I always reply to them because I remember once upon a time when I was very grateful because this man was so generous to me. If you're to be a critic, the thing you need most is some encouragement, some stimulus.

In the beginning of the 70s, *The Times* cut down on the quantity of reviews and I wrote to *The Guardian*. It so happened that the then *Guardian* critic was suffering periods of ill health and couldn't always go to the theatre, so they were looking for a replacement. Again it was a mixture of good fortune and encouragement. I happened to write to them in the right time but also their features editor Peter Preston, with whom I'd been at Oxford, knew my work well. So I joined the paper in 1971 and here we are – more than 25 years later – I'm still working on *The Guardian*.

JAMES CHRISTOPHER:

I went to Edinburgh University and, of course, I went to see the Festival and I got caught up with it. I started doing reviews for a student newspaper but in 1986, the last year of my studies, the newspaper folded. So I set up my own festival paper – sheets of A3, 1000 copies – and handed it out for 20p. There was a whole bunch of us doing this. We literally started with a photocopier. We went to all the strange East European stuff that was performed in the smaller venues. That's how I started.

Then I came down to London and became a decorator for two years. But since I'd always wanted to write, in 1987, I applied to *Time Out* and started off as their wine correspondent. I knew nothing about wine at all. But that's how I got a regular column in *Time Out*. Then I asked Jane Edwardes if she needed any freelance reviewers. She said, "Yes. Let's try you out. Go and see this play and write 50 words." It was a very tough thing to do. But I did it. I went to see the most ridiculous show I've ever seen, called *Spike*. It was so bad it was hysterical. Jane liked my review and gave me another, and another. In 1989 I was employed full-time to do theatre in *Time Out* and I gave up the wine column. You're encouraged there to write in any way you want and since it's the make-or-break publication for the fringe, you have a lot of power as well. That's a wonderful combination for a young critic.

In 1996 I was asked to write for *The Sunday Express*. The interesting thing in reviewing for a right-wing newspaper is that they're completely personality-led. They don't want you to review the shows but the major stars in them. So you have to change your style, which is a great challenge. ... So from the Edinburgh fringe I've moved to the West End.

MICHAEL COVENEY:

As schoolboys, my brother and I got involved in the local drama company in Essex. Anyone who wasn't in the play each month wrote a review and read it out to the people who were in the play. So you learned a good lesson: to say what you think to people you know. Then I went to university at Oxford where I wrote in the students' newspaper and took part in the students' theatre. When I left, I started script-reading at the Royal Court and teaching. Then, in 1972, I became the third-string theatre critic on *The Financial Times*. From 1975 to 1978 I was involved with *Plays and Players*. I was with *The Financial Times* for nearly 20 years – as a third-string critic until 1976, as a second-string one until 1981, and then as their first critic. In 1990 there was a change around and *The Observer's* theatre critic, who had been in the job for six years, wanted to go back to being a literary editor, so they asked me to work for them. At the same time Irving Wardle went to *The Independent on Sunday*. In 1997 I moved to *The Daily Mail*.

NICK CURTIS:

I got into criticism by doing English and Drama at university and a one-year course in journalism in Cardiff. Then, in 1989, I was offered a two-week placement on *Plays and Players* magazine. The person whom I was substituting for left and I took over as a deputy editor. I stayed there about three years, the last nine months of which I was an editor. Then I started freelancing for *Time Out* and *The Independent*. In 1993 *The Evening Standard* rang in and asked me whether I would do work for them. I've been with them since then.

NICHOLAS DE JONGH:

I find it very difficult to remember the time when I decided that I wanted to be a theatre critic. As a teenager I was very much caught up with what I believed to be the romance of theatre criticism: going to first nights and seeing these men who were always rushing out and next morning being able to read their experience of what I too had seen. That romance has now gone from the theatre and disgracefully almost all theatre critics take 24 hours to write their response.

I did a degree in English Language and Literature at University College in London. Then I came into criticism by accident. I had a bizarre wish to be a producer of radio drama but I failed narrowly to become a trainee at the BBC. They offered me a contract to do news and magazines at Bush House, which I did for six months. Then I got onto *The Guardian* amazingly: while I was unemployed after university, I wrote a piece about being unemployed and something else. *The Guardian* accepted those pieces and offered me a job in Manchester. I loathe Manchester, so I didn't go. *The Guardian* in London asked me to do a theatre review and I found it very exciting having to write in the night, by 11 o'clock. Six months later they offered me a job as a general reporter at *The Guardian* in London and I took it. Within a month the features editor asked me if I liked to do a review. It was about an orgy taking place in a theatre called The Open Space. So that's how I started doing little bits of reviewing. Then I became the arts reporter and arts correspondent – a sort of deputy critic for Michael Billington. I did that for far too long. Then, in 1991, I was lucky to escape to The *Evening Standard* as chief theatre critic. When I was at *The Guardian*, I did a M.Phil. degree on Jacobean Drama.

JANE EDWARDS:

I read drama at university and then was a founding member of a touring theatre company doing everything, as we all did. I became interested in working in one of the art centres where we were regularly playing and did a course in arts administration. After working as an administrator in a fringe theatre I knew I wanted to do something different and without really knowing what I was going to do I was lucky enough to be asked to do some freelance reviews for *Time Out*. So it was, at first, a way of earning money when I was broke, but I found I quite enjoyed doing it. Somehow the relationship with the theatre suited me. I liked having the broad view that came with seeing so much. Otherwise you become completely involved in your own company or you don't have time to go to the theatre or can't afford it.

After four years of freelance work for *Time Out* and other magazines, I got a full-time job at *Time Out* and I worked my way up. In 1985 I became Theatre editor. It's one of the best jobs. You are given a great deal of independence and you are doing a mixture of features and reviews. I don't have to go to the theatre every night because we have a team of reviewers at *Time Out,* and so I don't get worn down.

JOHN ELSOM:

I've always thought of myself being more of a writer than a critic. I was a regular reviewer and on the whole enjoying it but I would have enjoyed it much less if I hadn't been writing books and plays, and doing a little bit of directing and teaching as well. It was really a matter of trying to keep my eye on my main ideological goal, which was to look in the way which mythologies were being developed.

I had some plays and musicals on in the '50s. One of them nearly came to London and as a kind of compensation that it didn't the promoters invited me to join Paramount Pictures as a script-reader. So from 1960 onwards I had an opportunity to see nearly everything in the London theatres and not only that but also to recommend the actors and actresses. It was an extremely exciting time. I thought I ought to look at how society formed its group values – what I'd now call mythology. I was interested in the arts as being something expressing and developing a social mythology. In 1960 I started writing for the Third Programme of the BBC, for *Variety,* and I had a monthly column for *London Magazine* where I published my first critical pieces. At the end of the '60s I left Paramount in order to write my first book. It was about the repertory theatres. After the publication of the book I was invited to join *The Observer* as a second-string critic to Robert Brustein. After having written maybe half a dozen columns for them, I was asked to join the BBC as a critic for *The Listener.* During the course of the next 10–12 years several developments happened. I helped to get The Bush Theatre off the ground and we had a very successful run in promoting new plays there. I published more books, among them a book about the relations of men and women in the theatre and a book about The National Theatre. In the late '70s I was invited to write the arts policy manifesto of the Liberal Party and then I became Chair of their Arts and Broadcasting Committee for ten years (1978–1988). I left *The Listener* in 1982 and joined a non-market tabloid, *The Mail on Sunday,* for a year. In 1986 I joined the Department of Arts Policy and Management at City University, London, to develop a course of arts criticism within the Department of Arts Policy and Management because I was writing a lot about the economic climate of all the arts. In 1985 I was elected President of the IATC and stayed there until 1992. This was wonderful because it enabled me to see how British theatre related to the theatre in other countries. It made me realize the limitations of what we normally see in the West.

LYN GARDNER:

My parents went to the theatre a lot, so while most children's first memories are films, mine are of going to see theatre. Not necessarily great theatre, often touring productions, but by the time I was 10 I had certainly seen many shows. Then, in my early teens, I saw lots of shows at The National Theatre, the RSC and in the West End with friends. My parents were funding that. They were very encouraging. When I was at university, I wrote for the local paper and the student paper. Then I came to London and wrote for a number of small publications. In 1981 I got involved with the setting up of *City Limits* and I started covering everything on the fringe. Eventually I became a theatre reviewer there. *City Limits* was extremely influential in encouraging women critics. Without it we wouldn't have as many women critics as there are now. After *City Limits* I became a freelance critic. Then I was on maternity leave and in 1995 I went to the *The Guardian* as deputy to Michael Billington.

ROBERT GORE-LANGTON:

I have no family connections in the theatre whatsoever and I wasn't taken to the theatre as a kid. The first serious non-pantomime I ever saw was Alistair Sim in the early '60s in Chichester. I started wanting to be a chef and I trained as a chef but that didn't really agree with me because I couldn't stand the heat in the kitchen. Then I decided that I wanted to be an arts journalist. I wrote a letter to a group of arts magazines and a year later a man rang me up and said, "We are looking for an editorial assistant. Do you have any knowledge of publishing?" I said, "No." And he said, "Come in, come in." The next thing I knew was I had started working at one of their rather camp magazines – *Plays and Players*. I worked my way up from that position to being an editor within three years and that's where I cut my teeth on theatre. I discovered there what I did and didn't like about the theatre, and it got into my blood. I enjoyed the writing most of all. You've got to like writing – that's the key to it. But the magazine was very badly managed. It was dying in a way and I felt that there was nothing I could do about it but get out. So I took a decision to go freelance as a writer specializing in theatre. It took me a long time to find enough work. But I was very lucky: I had a wife who could earn some money. I started writing for *Time Out* and I did a little bit for *The Times*, *The Sunday Times*, and one or two other newspapers. Then, in 1989, I was approached by Charles Spencer who had just become the main theatre critic on *The Daily Telegraph*. He said, "Would you be interested in writing for *The Telegraph*?" I said, "Yuppee!!", and took the job, and stayed there for seven years. In 1996 I joined *The Sunday Express* as their theatre critic.

JOHN GROSS:

I became a critic by accident and I'm not, perhaps, a true member of the profession. I'm really a literary critic. That was my main job for many years. In the beginning of the '60s, I wrote a theatre column in a monthly magazine but only for about a year. Then in the '80s, when I was writing about books for *The New York Times*, I sometimes wrote about plays. But none of this makes me a theatre critic. In 1989 I came back to England and I was looking for a half-time job so as to leave me half a day for writing. By pure accident I met the editor-in-chief of *The Sunday Telegraph* and he said, "I need a new theatre critic. My old one's retired. Are you interested?" I said, "Well, I must tell you I'm not a professional critic. I have written about theatre and I'm extremely interested in it but there are many plays and productions I haven't seen." "Excellent!" – he said. "We don't want a member of the clique." When I told my daughter, who was in college, that I was going to do this job, she applauded and said, "Dad, you must get a cape and a cloak with red lining." I haven't, but I know what she means. When I started I was very wary that I was not one of the boys and girls and they were aware of that too. For a few months it was awkward but I enormously enjoyed doing my job and now that I've done it for many years, it's a habit.

BILL HAGERTY:

I've been in newspapers in London all my life. I was a deputy editor of *The Daily Mirror*. Then I became an editor of *The People*. In 1992, as often happens with editors, the management changed and I was dispensed with. So, as there were, and are, an awful lot of ex-editors on the street I had to re-invent myself. I've always been very interested in theatre and I've written little bits of theatre criticism over the years. So I was fortunate that I managed to persuade the paper *Today* to have a theatre column. After a while they invited me to be their film critic as well and it was great until the end of 1995 when the paper closed down. I then had to slightly re-invent myself again. I went to *News of the World* – the biggest-selling Sunday newspaper in the Western world – and they decided they'd like a theatre column. Not only because it was a service to the readers but they rather liked the idea that they'd get publicity outside the theatres. It gives them a little bit of class. So I'm a relatively new theatre critic but with a very long experience as a newspaper man.

PETER HEPPLE:

I'm a critic only by accident. Actually I wouldn't call myself a critic. I'm a reviewer and I've worked in publicity and public relations. I review plays because it's the best way of getting free tickets. I'm quite shameless about that. I'm interested in going to the theatre and if the price I have to pay is writing about it, so I'll write about it as well as I can. I'm probably unlike most critics. I'm interested in the mechanics of the business – not just theatre but show business on the whole. We are an entertainment conscious country but not necessarily theatre conscious country. At least not these days. I don't think the majority of the people who go to theatre are really serious about it. For them it's just a part of the entertainment business. It's a live show.

I've always been associated with *The Stage*. Until 1972 I was an outside contributor. My first reviews were about variety, which is something everybody in the office except me is too young to remember. Then, around 1953/54, I gradually switched to reviewing plays. Afterwards I became an editor of the paper.

IAN HERBERT:

I read Classics at Cambridge and did lots of theatre as a student. I acted, directed and wrote, but had just as much fun working the lighting switchboard for the great theatre-makers who were there in my time – people like Ian McKellen, Derek Jacobi, and Trevor Nunn. I said to myself, "If student actors are as good as this, what must the professionals be like?" and decided that the professional theatre was right out of my league. Undergraduate theatre was tough enough – I finished up doing cabaret and producing my own revues because I could be a bigger fish in this smaller pool.

From Cambridge I went to work in a large publishing house, where I became director of their general publishing. I was responsible for a wide-ranging list, including theatre books, among them *Who's Who in the Theatre*, which I kept going by editing it in my spare time. An American publisher then bought *Who's Who* and me with it, and for a couple of years I lived very well, until the Americans noticed they had a recession. Their first economy was the European office – which was me.

As an out of work publisher with some theatre knowledge, I tried with some friends to set up a theatre magazine – *Plays and Players* had just gone under – but nobody wanted to put up money for such a risky proposition. The only answer was to publish a theatre magazine that didn't need any money. I looked at the example of the great criminal and publisher Robert Maxwell, who had built a business from selling magazine subscriptions in advance, and it occurred to me that I could use the same technique.

As part of my *Who's Who* work I used a very interesting American publication, *New York Critics' Theatre Reviews*, which republished all the reviews of the Broadway critics. I thought I could do the same for London, with cast lists and the addition of extra information like what shows were coming up – a continuation of the factual recording work of *Who's Who*. The London critics said "Yes, that sounds a useful idea, we'll let you use our reviews." So in January 1981 I used the last thousand pounds I had in the bank to print and send out a thousand copies of *London Theatre Record* to everybody I could think of in English and overseas theatre saying, "Would you like to pay for a year of this service?" Enough of them said "Yes" to pay the next print bill, and so it has gone on ever since.

It was only after a couple of years of publishing the *Record* that I started adding my own editorial letter at the front. At first there was resistance, "Who is this man? What does he know about theatre?" But by then I'd seen several thousand productions all over the world and I decided that once you've seen that much theatre you're entitled to comment on it. Now that I've been doing it for more years than many of today's critics, people have got used to my interventions.

ROBERT HEWISON:

Unlike some theatre critics I have other interests in life. My main work is as a cultural historian but when I started I didn't have a university position to support my research. So I've been writing my books working as a broadcaster and as a literary journalist.

In 1981 I was writing book reviews for *The Times Literary Supplement*. One day the editor turned round to me and said, "Robert, would you like to review a film or a theatre?" I hesitated, and then said, "Theatre." So I went to the theatre, wrote a review, and then he said, "Would you like to write another one?" Then he said that *The Sunday Times* wanted me to telephone them. It so happened that James Fenton, the poet, was the drama critic on *The Sunday Times* at that time and John Peter, who'd been the deputy critic, didn't want to continue. So I went into that space and I have occupied it ever since. That's how I became a drama critic – quite by chance and not by choice.

It so happened that when I was at Oxford as an undergraduate, I was an actor and director, and I acted in a university production which was on in the West End (*Hang Down Your Head and Die*). In fact my first theatre criticism was to decide that I wasn't a very good actor. So I had a background of theatrical experience. Before I worked for newspapers I worked a lot for the BBC and I'd occasionally review plays. The interesting thing about the BBC was that although it's a very liberal organization, you had an editor sitting beside you in the theatre, as it were, mediating your experience. Whereas working for *The Sunday Times* is totally free: I go alone, review the show, and they put it in the newspaper. It's so much more direct than working with a corporation like the BBC. You have a position of trust. I'm also now a professor of cultural studies at Lancaster University. I regard being a theatre critic as something which energizes my academic studies.

JEREMY KINGSTON:

Although I did science at school, I acted in the school plays and I enjoyed that. We were close enough to London to come and go to the theatre. After school I went to the army and then instead of going to university, I came to London to start working. I worked a number of jobs, one of which was at the box-office of the Criterion Theatre in Piccadilly Circus when *Waiting for Godot* was on for the first time here. Every morning I would arrive for work at the stage door, go downstairs, and walk across the back of the stage. And there would be the set: twisted metal and a painted black board and a lamp underneath, which was going to shine the moon on the backdrop in the end of the act. I saw it a couple of dozen times and the magic worked again and again. It was the most powerful experience working there. Then, in 1957, I wrote a play – *No Concern of Mine*, sent it for *The Observer* competition and it was mentioned among the prize-winners.

In 1964 the *Punch* theatre critic had died and they were looking for somebody young. I didn't know this when I visited the man who had temporarily taken over. His son was a drama-student friend of another drama-student who was a lodger in my flat. It's a complicated story but we all went over to tea with this man: I talked about theatre and in the end he asked me if I'd like to be the theatre critic of *Punch*. These things hurtle out of the blue. When people ask me how to become a theatre critic, I suggest they write some reviews and send them to *Time Out*, and then work their way up because that's how it usually happens. But I didn't do that. I was suddenly given 800 words a week and I stayed on doing that for 10 years. In those days one person was able to cover the majority of plays that were on not only in London but in Manchester, Stratford, etc. While I was working there I had a second play on in West End – *Signs of the Time*. In 1975 I was sacked and I then wrote a series of illustrated coffee-table books on various subjects, like theatre, medicine and exploration. Then my wife and I went to live in the country where I worked for some printers, wrote radio plays and talks for radio, and wrote TV plays.

In 1985 one of the theatre critics on *The Times* died and I wrote to the arts editor suggesting myself. For a while I alternated with somebody else and in 1986 I took over as No. 2 to Irving Wardle, and now No. 2 to Benedict Nightingale, which I've been doing ever since. Meanwhile I was a restaurant critic for six years for *What's On*. That's it: all my life I've never been simply one thing or another sexually, creatively or intellectually. It's been arts and science, critic **and** creator.

ALASTAIR MACAULAY:

I'm a farmer's son. Every man in my family was a farmer. My brothers are farmers. My mother comes from a farming family. But I was the sickly child of the family. I was ill with asthma, so I grew up with records and reading books. I've always loved the performing arts. When I was 20, in 1976, I fell particularly in love with dance; and, when I came to London, I wrote letters about every dance performance I went to. I read classics at university – Latin and Greek. I was never trained as a journalist and I had no personal expertise on dance or notion of wanting to be a critic. When I left university, I wanted to act. But I didn't do anything about it because I was too busy going to the theatre every night. Some of my friends said, "You should be a critic. You are writing these letters, so you're already half-way there." I was lucky: when I was 22, I got my first job for a minor magazine and very soon, to my surprise, I realized I loved the whole business of trying to discuss and describe performances. I thought it was what God had put me on this earth to do. And I still feel that way.

In 1988, I began working for *The Financial Times* as their second dance critic. Then they asked me what else I could do; and I started doing some music criticism, despite having very little formal music training. That was a privilege, because I believe that music is the holy art – the art that most readily puts you in touch with the sublime. In 1990, I started doing theatre as well. Since 1994, I've been in charge of *The Financial Times'* theatre coverage; and I now cover dance and music in my spare time.

SHERIDAN MORLEY:

I grew up as the son and grandson of actors. My mother's mother, Dame Gladys Cooper, was a famous London theatre actress in the '20s and the first woman to run a commercial theatre there. My father, Robert Morley, was an actor who spent most of his life in the West End theatre, made about a hundred movies and was in many plays. So I've always been interested in the theatre. I was taken to the theatre from the age of five, not only in England but all around the world. I was with my parents on a tour to America and Australia for about five years and I did some child acting in Australia, but the only thing that I discovered, as did the Australians, was that I couldn't really act. I had a lot of student experience of acting and directing. In Oxford, as a student actor, I worked in lots of student theatre. In 1962, when I was 21, I had a wonderful chance to go to America, to the University of Hawaii, and helped to run their student theatre for a year.

Gradually I discovered that I loved talking about the performance and that I was able to describe plays and explain why people should go and see them, and sometimes equally important – why they should not go. So when I came back to England, I knew I wanted to be a critic. But couldn't find the way in. I became a newscaster in TV. From there I went into the BBC TV as an interview-host and did about seven years of that. When the show (*Late Night Line Up*) closed, I went to *The Times* but not writing criticism because they had a very good theatre critic – Irving Wardle. I went on the feature side doing interviews. That's something I've always done and still do on TV. In 1975 I became the arts editor and drama critic of *Punch*, which I did for 15 years, mainly writing about plays. At that time I was asked to join the *International Herald Tribune* where I've now been for 20 years writing the theatre column. When *Punch* closed, I went to the BBC Radio and TV and began again to make my life as a broadcaster which I still do. In 1990 I joined the *Spectator*.

So most of my adult life I've made at least a half of my living as a critic. But critics have a very hard time making their living in this country. The papers pay very highly for sports writers or for political columnists but not for theatre critics who are assumed to have a rather nice life: you go to the theatre, you get your tickets free ... That's why most of us do other jobs. In my case I have my radio shows at the BBC, I do a theatre show on TV in the winters, I've done 20 books and I teach at BADA (the British-American Drama Academy). We divide into the academics and the performers. I belong to the second group. I do one-man shows and speeches, and I write two-hander musicals and little tiny shows. I've always believed the critic has to be a practitioner as well.

DAVID NATHAN:

The only family influence was that my mother was crazy about the theatre, particularly the musical theatre. We lived in Manchester and whenever she had the chance, we'd go to one of the two main theatres. She had a good voice and she knew all the songs from the old shows, and used to sing them. So I still know the words of old musicals probably no-one even remembers. When I was 15 years old I left school and started work as a messenger at *The News Chronicle*. Later I became a general reporter on a paper in Nottingham. They had a good theatre critic but he became ill and they appointed a woman. She was also a good theatre critic but she became pregnant. They knew I used to go to the theatre and asked me to start covering it as a part-time job. Then I came to London and joined *The Daily Herald* as a reporter and feature writer, and travelled abroad a lot. Once there was a very bad air crash at Gatwick and I beat another reporter in the race to the only telephone a mile down the lane. I was about 30 and I thought, "I'm not going to do this when I'm 40. I want to do something else." So I decided to start concentrating on theatre. The critic on *The Daily Herald* was also a general news reporter and when he went to cover some foreign war I took over as the critic. I was also the chief entertainment writer. I stayed there until the paper closed down in 1969.

That was a turning point in my life. I was 42 years old. I had a wife and two children, and a large mortgage. I had also just written my first novel and Bryan Forbes, head of film productions at E.M.I. Studios Elstree, commissioned me to write a screen-play based on it. I did the first draft, Bryan liked it and paid me the second installment of the fee. Everything was going extremely well even though I had no newspaper to write for. Then Forbes was fired and all his production plans were scrapped. *The Jewish Chronicle* had asked me to become their theatre critic when the old paper folded. I had turned it down at the time as I had two other books, a biography and an investigation into comedy by talking to comedians and writers, to write. So I asked them if they were still interested in me as a theatre critic. "No," they said, "We'd be interested in you as an arts editor *and* critic." I accepted their offer. Then I became deputy editor but I always kept my theatre column. Now that I've retired I still do interviews and write reviews for them. I also write for *Applause*, *Prospect* and other journals.

BENEDICT NIGHTINGALE:

I was brought up in Kent, so we used to go to the theatre in London quite a lot and I got obsessed with it. When I got older and could travel by myself, I used to come to London on Fridays and see three plays on Saturday. At that stage I wanted to become an actor. I acted a great deal at school. I played all the leading parts – Shaw's *Cleopatra*, Prince Hal in *Henry IV*. I thought that to be an actor was very exciting but I realized I wasn't very good at it. I used to take all theatre magazines and when I graduated I found a job on a paper in Kent. They invited me to do a bit of local drama reviewing. There was a weekly repertory company and I remember the first thing I ever reviewed. I was too hard on it: I said it was like a pudding, and someone called the paper and said I mustn't be so rude.

I went further into journalism at the university in Cambridge. I read English because theatre or drama didn't really exist as subjects in the English universities at that time. I edited the university newspaper, did some reviewing and a little acting. David Hare, Trevor Nunn, and Ian McKellen were there at that time too. Then I went to America for a year on a scholarship.

When I came back, I joined *The Guardian* in the North of England as a general journalist. I wrote about loads of things but also about the theatre and quite rapidly they made me the northern theatre critic. I used to write under quite difficult circumstances: two or three times a week I'd review plays for the next day's paper. I lived for a while in Manchester but when I got married we moved to London and I started doing freelance theatre journalism. In 1968 I was invited to become a theatre critic at *The New Statesman* and worked on it, on and off, for nearly 18 years with another period in America in between. I was writing a lot for *The New York Times* from London and when Walter Kerr left as the Sunday critic, they asked me over to be the Sunday critic for a bit. So I did it for a year (1983/84) leaving my family behind here. Then I decided I couldn't move the family completely over there and I took up an academic job at the University of Michigan, which allowed me to be half of the year there and half of the year here. I was teaching English Literature and Drama, and organized a M.F.A. course in criticism. Then *The Times* offered me this job and I joined the paper on January 1st 1990. So I've been there ever since and I still do some articles for *The New York Times*. This is really what I wanted to do. I didn't really feel comfortable being an academic. When I was a weekly critic for *The New Statesman*, I used to do a lot of radio reviewing too but I do it much less now.

JOHN PETER:

I got interested in the idea of criticism when I was a post-graduate at Oxford. An undergraduate friend of mine was writing reviews for *The Times*. I was working on my post-graduate dissertation about Elizabethan and Jacobean drama, so I was soaked in theatre ideas, and when this friend of mine left, I applied to *The Times*. I was interviewed and they tried me out with a few short pieces on university productions. That's how I started. I then applied and was accepted for a permanent job as a reporter and editorial assistant on *The Times Educational Supplement*, where I served my three-year apprenticeship, from 1964 till 1967. I was very lucky to have got this because I was able to work in London and see a lot of theatre. I continued to do free-lance criticism more and more frequently for *The Times*. Then I got a job as an editorial assistant on *The Sunday Times* literary and arts department, which edited the books and the arts pages, and also did some theatre reviewing. The No. 1 critic was Harold Hobson. He was succeeded by Bernard Levin and he in turn – by James Fenton. I succeeded James Fenton in 1984.

IAN SHUTTLEWORTH:

I studied Law and then English at Cambridge, and I did a lot of acting and some journalism as a student. I then heard about the National Student Drama Festival. In 1988 it came to Cambridge and I went alone since I wasn't with any show. I fell absolutely in love with the Festival's atmosphere. I was like a young boy who had been to the carnival for the first time and would want to run away with the show when it left the town. When the following year I won the Student Critic of the Year Award, a friend suggested that I tried to use that award to get some Edinburgh work. I got work with *The Independent*. It had its own Festival Award and I was basically running around like a mad thing, seeing as many shows as possible, and referring to the real reviewers and the award judges the shows that I thought were worthwhile. In 1990 I went back to Edinburgh – this time as a full reviewer and on the award panel. One of the other judges was Lyn Gardner – the theatre editor of *City Limits*. A couple of months later – in the autumn of 1990 – I finally left Cambridge and moved to London. Lyn Gardner started giving me little bits of reviewing work for *City Limits* – not enough to make a living, but enough to keep my hand in. I occasionally got to do some short reviews in *The Independent* too. In 1991 Lyn Gardner went off on maternity leave and asked me to sit in for her at *City Limits*. The magazine then changed editorship three times during the next six months and at some stage the new regime decided they didn't want Lyn back, so I took the job on permanently. I'm not proud of having let Lyn be treated so shabbily, but in the end I didn't oppose it. They also decided to give the book section to me. I was with *City Limits* until it folded in 1993. Then I drifted sideways into freelance work with various magazines. I did some work on *The Evening Standard* and when its arts editor moved to *The Financial Times*, she began to give me regular work there.

I've never in my life got a journalistic job through applying and being interviewed. It has all been a combination of contacts in the right place and in the right time.

CHARLES SPENCER:

I drifted into criticism purely by accident. I read English at Oxford and I couldn't think of what I wanted to do as a career. I joined the local paper in Guildford, Surrey, and did a bit of everything – court reporting, council meetings, etc. Because I had done English as a degree they wanted me to do theatre criticism as well. This was in the mid '70s and it was a good place to start. There were three theatres in Surrey. I was reviewing them and then I started to review the RSC and The National Theatre. I also started doing film and I became their arts specialist. Then, in 1979, I went to *The Evening Standard* as the No. 3 critic and arts reporter, and I did some feature writing as well. I didn't enjoy my time there and had a sort of nervous breakdown. So in 1984 I went to *The Stage* as a sub-editor and went on reviewing. In 1986 I joined the London *Daily News*. When it folded a year later, I joined *The Daily Telegraph* as one of the sub-editors on the arts page and as the deputy theatre critic doing two or three shows a week. In early 1991, my predecessor got the push and I got his job. So though I've been reviewing plays on and off since 1976, I've only been doing it full-time since 1991.

I learned how to be a critic by doing it. To me it's an entirely practical and instinctive job rather than something you should have any theories about. I see myself first and foremost as a working journalist rather than an academic, or as a part of the theatre scene. I don't have a lot of dogmatic beliefs or theories. One of my few beliefs is that it's very important that theatre critics don't get too close to the people they are working with.

JACK TINKER:

I was born in the North of England in a tiny little town – Royton. When I was about three I was first taken to the theatre. After the show they took me backstage and I became totally absorbed by the creation of illusion: how a flat painted bit of canvas became the Mediterranean sky, for instance, was a miracle for me. I totally believed what I saw on stage. And then to be shown that it was make-believe was shattering. I started going to the theatre regularly when I was about eight. We had a very good repertory company and I also went to Manchester to see as much as I could afford to. At that time in London there was this wonderful explosion of new theatre with Pinter, Wesker, Beckett, Osborne, and theatre was news. There were also some wonderful critics: Kenneth Tynan, Harold Hobson, and Bernard Levin, and, of course, the only way I knew what was going on there was by reading those men. So, when I was about 12, I decided I wanted to be a critic. I thought that the only difference between them and me was that I paid every penny I got to go to the theatre and they got paid to go to the theatre.

I must have been 14 when we all had to write pin-portraits of each other for the school magazine, and Ben Chapman, now a deputy editor in *The Daily Express*, had written a portrait of me and had called it *Tinker – the Critic*. So, obviously, I had established then what I was going to be. When I was actually asked what I wanted to be, I'd said I wanted to be Bernard

Levin. I had a wonderful English head master who kept telling me that I wrote journalistically, which I thought was a great compliment because I wanted to be a journalist. The school had three Oxbridge scholarships and they were quite sure that I was going to get one, but he kept saying I'd never get it with this style. Once he sent one of my essays to the Manchester paper and they not only accepted it but asked me to write a column for them. The column was called *For the Under 21s By the Under 21s*. Then they offered me a job in their branch office. I had huge fights with everybody including my headmaster and I finally left but I realized that I'd made a terrible mistake. I thought, "I'm trying to be a journalist but how do I become a critic?"

Then I went to Brighton where I knew there was a huge theatre centre and a very good evening paper. I was about 19. And one of these magical pieces of luck happened. Shortly after my arriving there, the theatre critic made a huge mistake by panning a show called *Beyond the Fringe* which went on to become the most successful revue of the year. So he left and I became their theatre critic. I stayed there for eight years. At that time all the major producers tried plays out at the Theatre Royal there. I got letters from people like Joe Orton and met people like Terence Rattigan. I gave a dreadful review to a new play of Rattigan and he invited me around, and gave me a master class in theatre construction going through the play line by line. Then I met Marlene Dietrich. She rang the office up to thank me for a review and asked whether I'd like to see the show again. Something had gone wrong with the show and I had to tell her what I thought had gone wrong. I thought the songs were too different and she didn't give the audience time to readjust its focus. She thought for a moment and said, "Do you know that the boy is right? There was a long introduction to that song, and I had skipped it." That gave me so much courage and confidence because if you can tell someone like Dietrich to her face what's wrong with her act, you must never fake a review. You must never ever be even slightly dishonest in reviews. Trust that sort of tune in yourself, which is all that you've got. At 21 I was young but I had an awful lot of knowledge and confidence.

Then I was invited by *The Daily Sketch* to go to America and edit their gossip column. I didn't want to do that because I didn't know anything about gossip columns but the editor – Sir David English – said that this was going to be a first step to becoming a theatre critic. I said I thought I was a theatre critic already. In the end, for a year I edited the gossip column under the name of Richard Rolf, filling in with reviews at the same time. In 1972 the paper folded and David English became the editor of *The Daily Mail*, and totally reorganized it. He kept his promise and made me his theatre critic. He took theatre from a sort of ghetto and moved it to the third page of news and gave me a terribly high profile. So I've been incredibly lucky.

IRVING WARDLE:

I was glamorized by literary criticism when I was a boy. It seemed very glamorous to be able to have an independent viewpoint and have it published. But I didn't intend to be doing it for a living. I wanted to do music. I went to Oxford, then I went into the army, and then to the Royal College of Music where I discovered I would never make a living out of music.

I had a godfather who edited a newspaper in my home-town Bolton, Lancashire. He happened to know the guy who was editing the arts page in *The Times*, they gave me a try, and I started writing little notices. It was an amazing leap: from zero to be writing for *The Times*! It happened because there was nothing else in prospect but it was intoxicating and flattering. I started working as a sub-editor on one of the supplements of *The Times* on education and was writing notices at night. I had a few jolly years. Rubbish was the norm in the West End in those days and it was a pleasure saying so, and figuring you were helping clear space for maybe better things to come in. Then the new playwriting movement got going. The magazine *Encore* was another place to write for. They didn't pay but it was a great pleasure writing for them because the only reason was that you had something to say.

In 1959 I got the opportunity to go to *The Observer*, which was a dream of mine because it was a wonderful publication. It was like the aristocracy of journalism. The leading theatre reviewer was, of course, Kenneth Tynan whom I was fascinated by. There he was suddenly a colleague! He was very nice and friendly, because I was taking a bit of weight off his back by going to all things he didn't want to see. It was frustrating because he was never going to tell how much he's going to write, so I might start with 400 words and finish with 70 in print. I was at *The Observer* for three years. Then I went back to *The Times* and stayed there for 27 years. Everything in my life used to last three years in those days: university courses, jobs, marriages. And suddenly it was a long spell.

MATT WOLF:

When I was a teenager, everyone thought I'd become an academic. I did English at Yale university and when I graduated in 1983, I planned to go on with my studies – to get an M.A. degree and then a Ph.D. I got into all the places I applied but wanted to go for a break before I continued. So I decided I'd come to Britain for six months on a student work visa, do whatever I could, save up my pennies, and go to the theatre. I thought if I could get some journalistic work, so much the better because then it could be some helpful experience if I wanted to pursue journalism in America. So I wrote letters to various places in Britain from New York. The first place on my list was the Associated Press and when I arrived in London, I called them up and met with the chief editor. "We don't have anybody regularly doing theatre, so do you have any ideas for a story?" – he asked me. "Certainly!" – I said. The same week David Mamet had the world premiere of *Glengarry Glen Ross* at The National Theatre, so with the arrogance of youth, I called the press officer and said, "This is Matt Wolf, AP. I want to interview David Mamet." I did the interview, wrote the piece, brought it to the AP, and when they said they'd buy it, I was astonished. They gave me fifty pounds for it and asked if I had any other stories. So AP became my base. It wasn't a full-time job but the money was enough. But I didn't just want to write for the AP and I did a thing that apparently you don't do in Britain: I wrote letters to some British publications saying I wanted to be a theatre critic. The economy was blooming and there were many publications that had a lot of space. So I started writing for *City Limits, Plays and Players, Drama* magazine and *The Listener*.

At the end of the six months I extended my work permit for another six months. Then I said to myself, "I'm actually not very interested in going to graduate school." I decided I wanted to make a go as a theatre journalist. It was my great passion at Yale. I used to do a lot of reviewing in the school paper and the summer of 1983 I was a critic at the Eugene O'Neill Playwrights' Conference in Connecticut. So I was beginning to think even then, "Hm-m-m, this is the sort of thing I can imagine as a life." In 1984 I called the European edition of *The Wall Street Journal* in Brussels, introduced myself and said that I had an idea for a story. That's how I started doing stuff for them and about a year and a half later they asked me if I'd be their theatre critic. I couldn't believe that: to be the critic of *The Wall Street Journal/ Europe*! So, of course, I said, "Yes, please!" It was a great complement to the AP job. That continued for six years. Then in 1992 *The Wall Street Journal* laid off all their European arts writers. As luck would happen, just then *Variety* was looking for a new theatre critic in London and they asked me if I was interested in the job. It was perfect! Initially I was hired to do the reviews, then after about two years they asked me to take over the column every other week. So now I do the column, reviews and features for them, and it's actually a much greater chunk of my life than the AP. But I'm still very devoted to the AP because they did take me in off the street and I'll never forget that. Also, they have a lot of integrity and that can't always be said for Fleet Street. I also try to do as much freelance work as I can without dragging myself to an early grave ... So having come for 6 months, I've been here more than 14 years.

2

HATS OFF TO THE MASTERS: WHO MADE CRITICS WANT TO BE CRITICS?

Kate Bassett	**Sheridan Morley**
Michael Coveney	**Benedict Nightingale**
Nick Curtis	**John Peter**
Nicholas de Jongh	**Ian Shuttleworth**
Lyn Gardner	**Jack Tinker**
John Gross	**Matt Wolf**

They answer the question:

– *Who do you consider your mentor in theatre criticism?*

KATE BASSETT:

I don't have a mentor. It would be slightly unhealthy to have one, wouldn't it? There are reviewers who I admire for their perceptiveness and skill as writers. Many of them – like Benedict Nightingale, Charles Spencer, Paul Taylor – have been very supportive and helpful – at odds with the reputation of theatre critics as backbiting. Michael Billington was extremely kind when I was just starting out. He gave a lecture to the students on my M.A. course and I wrote him a letter asking if he could give me any advice on becoming a reviewer. He met me, paid for lunch too I seem to remember, and was incredibly helpful even though he didn't know me from Adam.

MICHAEL COVENEY:

I'm of the age when Kenneth Tynan was the great inspiration. He made theatre so sexy and important, and he was a genuine intellectual. So he was my idol really. I still think he was the best writer. I was too young to read him in the '50s. I caught up with him later – in the '60s, when I was at school. He was very kind to me when I started. Since then the people whose careers are exemplary to me are Irving Wardle and Michael Billington . . . I like a lot of American critics very much. I admire the witty criticism of George J. Nathan. Stark Young was a very impressive critic. Harold Clurman. Robert Brustein. I still take great pleasure reading them. Especially when I feel down about the job because they made it seem important and worthwhile.

NICK CURTIS:

My mentors tend to be critics from other media. Sometimes TV critics . . . Among the theatre critics I admire Nicholas de Jongh, Paul Taylor, and Benedict Nightingale. And I very much liked Jack Tinker. I admire hard critics who are prepared to be tough. There's no point of being soft on things. Nick and Paul are prepared to tell it as it is and not go easy on things. Benedict is one of the most eminent and intellectual critics working at the moment. But I wouldn't necessarily model myself on any of those four. That's a rather futile way of going about things. You should never try to emulate anyone else's writing style.

NICHOLAS DE JONGH:

When I was young, I was very much influenced by Irving Wardle. I admired his style, his seriousness, and his ability to convey the essence of the action on stage and analyze the author's intentions and the play's values. I admired Bernard Shaw for his witty capacity to make a performance live. I admire Eric Bentley.

LYN GARDNER:

It's easy to cull up all the great names such as Kenneth Tynan. In some ways I do think the excitement from reading Tynan in my teens was useful. But in a way it made me want to be a practitioner, it didn't make me think, "Oh, I must be a theatre critic!" Actually it took me quite a long time to have the courage to think that what I thought and felt had value, to discover that I had opinions. Sometimes I'm quite astonished by the self-confidence of some young critics . . . So nobody was actually my mentor. Far greater influences were my contemporaries, women like Ros Asquith, who was the theatre editor of *City Limits* and who encouraged me.

JOHN GROSS:

Hazlitt and Bernard Shaw are my ideals. Other critics who have impressed me are George Henry Lewes of the 19th century, Stark Young, Eric Bentley, and Kenneth Tynan. On the whole I like the colourful critics who are theatrical themselves.

SHERIDAN MORLEY:

Kenneth Tynan. He made many of us want to be critics. He was the first one to make the critic a star . . .

BENEDICT NIGHTINGALE:

I've always thought I had to make my own way without too many mentors. But at the time I started we were all under the influence of Kenneth Tynan who seemed to speak up for our generation. At school I used to take *The Observer* religiously and I recall going to see *Look Back in Anger* which Tynan had shown us why it was important. He had this capacity to express things in a robust, direct, concentrated and highly entertaining way. Someone else I do admire is Robert Brustein in the US. He's kept a sort of seriousness in criticism alive over a very long period.

JOHN PETER:

Irving Wardle. He was the first professional theatre critic whom I met. I didn't get to meet Kenneth Tynan, who was everybody's hero as well as mine until much later. By the time I met Irving, Tynan had given up theatre criticism. Irving encouraged me and it was through his recommendation that I was considered for the job on *The Times Educational Supplement*. I respect him tremendously for his complete and utter integrity and dedication to his profession. He is one of the very few people who can combine complete seriousness with readability, which is very important.

IAN SHUTTLEWORTH:

When I was a student and was making the decision to switch from Law to English, it was Kenneth Tynan who really fired me. The Student Drama Critic Award was given to me by Robert Hewison. He has kept an eye on me ever since. While I've never directly worked with Michael Coveney, he's always taken an interest in what I'm doing. He was quite concerned to find me a proper job in the period after *City Limits*. He'd been in *The Financial Times* and I had thought it would be nice if I could end up there. Those are the people I behold with due respect. But generally it's been everybody who's been around: Sarah Hemming took me under her wing at *The Independent* during the Edinburgh years, then Lyn Gardner at *City Limits*. I owe everything to someone or other.

JACK TINKER:

Bernard Levin was one of my mentors. He made theatre available and exciting to the man in the street. Which I think is part of my job. If you work for a paper which sells up to 3 million copies, you have to make it exciting and readable.

MATT WOLF:

When I was a teenager my critical mentor was the film critic Pauline Kael of *The New Yorker*. She wrote with such a mature intelligence and passion! And she was fearless! She was not afraid to say that something was shit and she wouldn't put up with it. But she also wasn't afraid to say that although everyone else thought something was shit she loved it. I'm often alone in my opinions here and I hope I'm as fearless as she is. . . . A critic whom I wouldn't call a mentor, but certainly someone I admire is Frank Rich. He's a fantastic writer and very much in Kael's style. He has exceptional knowledge and enthusiasm. On this side of the Atlantic, Benedict Nightingale and Paul Taylor are people who write beautifully. In fact I've kept Benedict's farewell piece from *The New Statesman*. It was so well written! It's wonderful to read the old critics as well – Shaw and James Agate, Harold Hobson and Kenneth Tynan. It's great here because you feel there's a literary tradition much more so than in the US.

3
"LIKE A WINE-WRITER IN BORDEAUX": REFLECTIONS FROM PARADISE

Michael Coveney
Nick Curtis
Nicholas de Jongh
John Elsom
Robert Gore-Langton
Ian Herbert
Alastair Macaulay
Sheridan Morley

Benedict Nightingale
John Peter
Ian Shuttleworth
Charles Spencer
Jack Tinker
Irving Wardle
Matt Wolf

They answer the question:

— American critics and theatre-makers alike say that their ideal for theatre criticism is the work of the London critics. How do you feel about being so regarded and respected?

MICHAEL COVENEY:

Americans are always saying that. They are always kowtowing to the British in a curious way: they bow down before the London theatre and then they hate us because of Andrew Lloyd Webber taking over the Broadway theatre. They think we're probably civilized and decent people, whereas they think their critics are a lot of cheap-shots. I don't think they're quite right. There's fine critics in America too. I like Mel Gussow and Jack Kroll. I used to like Frank Rich. There's no one like John Simon here but he is a fine critic. He disgusts me sometimes but he's very passionate.

NICK CURTIS:

It feels great! I love it. It's a terrific job. The really important and sometimes quite difficult thing is to maintain an enthusiasm for the job. I wanted to do it for ten years and now I've done it for seven years, but I think I'll carry on a bit.

NICHOLAS DE JONGH:

I understand why American theatre critics would say that. It's because of the overwhelming power of *The New York Times* to make or break a play. I'd hate to be in that position. I think it's healthy to have a situation in which we are a part of a process and no one of us has overwhelming power. That is very fortunate indeed.

JOHN ELSOM:

In this country it's nice to be a writer because you write for a public which is sophisticated about the use of the English language. It's nice to be able to say things in a way which would be completely missed in the States. When I write for an American magazine, I always have to put on a slightly heavier make-up and make the gestures much broader.

ROBERT GORE-LANGTON:

To say that London is the Mecca of brilliant theatre criticism is very nice but I simply don't know what to measure it against. We're a very small community which is doing a worthwhile job but there's good and there's bad, and I don't feel that I'm a part of some sort of a chosen race.

IAN HERBERT:

I think we are very lucky. I wouldn't want to be doing it anywhere else.

ALASTAIR MACAULAY:

Oh my God! My favorite job was in New York. I had a wonderful job on *The New Yorker*, I was their dance critic twice – in 1988 and 1992, for 6 months each time. *The New Yorker* was the ideal place to work for an essayist; and New York was the ideal place for dance, because dance is better than theatre there. I've learnt more from American critics than from British critics – on several different arts – and I've always felt that the highest standards are best expressed in New York. Moral standards. Nonetheless, London is the best place for theatre. Seeing great plays by authors whom we've hardly known before like Lope de Vega or Horvath – that's an immense privilege and yet it happens in London all the time. And a fair amount of impressive new plays as well!

SHERIDAN MORLEY:

We are very lucky. Being a critic in London is like being a wine-writer in Bordeaux. It's like being an Olympic Games writer in the town where the Olympics take place. If you are a critic in London, you can review five shows a week every week of the year.

BENEDICT NIGHTINGALE:

If you did my job you wouldn't think that was always so ideal. It has its ups and downs. But actually I feel very good about being a critic in the present time here. What's better about it is that there is much more varied product – more classical and new work. The reasons for that primarily have to do with the existence of public subsidy and national institutions such as the RSC and The National Theatre. In my year working in New York I reviewed one Shakespeare play, and that was *Henry V* in the Park. One Shakespeare play in an entire year! Here I review Shakespeare every other week. I go to the theatre four times a week and still don't keep up with the theatre fully. In New York I went to the theatre once or twice a week, and I more than kept up with it. Another obvious thing is that the theatre here is all-year round. So it just feels more worthwhile.

JOHN PETER:

We are lucky for several reasons. The US doesn't have national newspapers, whereas the London national newspaper critics have a national readership and there is an awareness that when you review a play in Liverpool people in London will read it and the other way around. Secondly, if you lined up the national newspaper critics, you'd get a group of people who are very different in terms of age, social background, sexual orientation, education, politics, life-style. If we all say that a play is a masterpiece, it's very likely to be quite good, and if we all say the play is rubbish, then you probably need not bother to go. In New York the success or failure of plays doesn't depend on word of mouth; in the British theatre the word-of-mouth factor is very important. People form their own opinions and pass them on. It's like a debate with the critics. But of course, I think we are all frightfully clever ...

IAN SHUTTLEWORTH:

I have what for me is an ideal job, yes! I get to see shows for free. I get to be an opinionated git and I get paid for it. That's perfect! But from a cultural perspective what the Americans say is the syndrome of the grass is always greener on the other side of the hill. They see the plurality and a certain amount of freedom here. The best example is *The Evening Standard*: Nicholas de Jongh took the critic's job there on the understanding that at no stage would he ever have to modify his political or social outlooks. That, of course, cuts both ways. Within the arts pages one has freedom but, because the arts are seen as a ghetto within the papers as a whole, that little freedom does not amount to a great deal in broad terms. We are perfectly free to go to the end of our little niches. But that's it.

CHARLES SPENCER:

There's no better town in the world to be a theatre critic – just because there's a terrific variety of theatre. We have a fantastic choice and that's what we thrive on. It's probably why we can't be experts. You've got to be able to do musicals one night, a comedian the next one, then a fringe show and Shakespeare.

JACK TINKER:

Oh, it's wonderful. I often think I can't believe my luck being in the right place at the right time AND in London. And being in a paper I wanted precisely to be on. It's just incredible! I'm very glad that I'm not in New York. And I'm certainly glad I'm not a critic for *The New York Times*. That kind of power is silly and absurd. It's almost obscene. It's not the fault of the critic there, it's the fault of New York audiences who look on failure like a disease and don't want to be any part of it. Here we have a far more independently minded public.

IRVING WARDLE:

I'm not sure they really mean that. It's common to belittle New York theatre criticism: "There's just one guy there! What a dreadful situation!" But at the same time Brits are tempted to go and do it, like Clive Barnes, and Benedict Nightingale. And the lecturing that goes with it.

To be a critic in London feels a routine job. The stuff comes through the post. You get out of the house at 5 o'clock thinking, "Am I going to find somewhere to park?" In the theatre you are thinking, "What time is this bloody thing going to finish?! Do they realize we've got to write tonight?" When it finishes you drive back, get the thing written somehow, smoke too much, have large whiskeys and collapse into insensibility till the next day. At the end of my book about criticism I quote a meeting with a French farmer who asked me what I did for a living. I said, "Theatre criticism." "I suppose that must exist!", he said, shrugging.

MATT WOLF:

It's wonderful being a critic in a country where theatre is taken seriously and in a city where you can see *The Phoenician Women* one night, *John Gabriel Borkman* the next one, and then *Hedda Gabler*. It doesn't matter that I didn't get my Ph.D. because you get it here by going to the theatre. I'll never forget when *The Phantom of the Opera* opened here in 1986: it was sandwiched in-between a production of *Ghosts* with Vanessa Redgrave and a production of *Misalliance*, and it was just another opening. Whereas when it opened in New York in January 1988, it was the only Broadway opening that month. Having said that, there's a quality of buzz and excitement about theatre in New York that London could benefit from. There's nothing like being at a show in New York that everyone wants to be at. You can feel the electricity in the air ... What I like about my position here is that I've reached the point where I can be an advocate for work from Britain to travel. I've helped some shows, like *Les Parents Terribles* and *An Inspector Calls* to get to New York. Another great thing about being a critic here is going to Ireland.

4

TO BE OR NOT TO BE REBORN
AS A CRITIC?
(AN INVITATION FOR
A LIFE ENCORE)

Michael Billington
James Christopher
Michael Coveney
Nicholas de Jongh
Robert Gore-Langton
Ian Herbert
Robert Hewison
Jeremy Kingston

Alastair Macaulay
Sheridan Morley
David Nathan
Benedict Nightingale
Ian Shuttleworth
Charles Spencer
Irving Wardle

They answer the question:

– If you were to start all over again, would you become a critic?

MICHAEL BILLINGTON:

Yes. Partly because it's the only job which I have the sense of being reasonably well-equipped for. I feel relatively at ease and confident when I'm sitting at a desk writing. The rest of life I find very confusing and difficult. There's an aesthetic pleasure in feeling that you may express what you want as clearly as you can. I love that. I also do love going to the theatre. And there's many benefits that one doesn't talk about enough. One does make good friends. For instance, Irving Wardle is someone I wouldn't have met had it not been for my profession. It takes you to interesting places and to countries you wouldn't go to otherwise. It also has a pleasant rhythm to it. Your evening is obviously committed but your daytime you can organize in your own way. I dread the thought of ever having a job which commands you to be at the desk at 9 o'clock in the morning. Sometimes I look out of my window on a Monday morning and watch people with briefcases going to offices, and I think, 'Thank God, I never joined that society!"

JAMES CHRISTOPHER:

Yes, I would become a critic. But not necessarily a theatre critic. It would be interesting if critics were encouraged to criticize and review other media as well. Undiluted theatre can be too constricting, and too narrow-minded. We should be able to write about other forms of theatre, like opera, football matches, or the government.

MICHAEL COVENEY:

Of course not. No! To start now is much harder. In those days you could live in London for twenty pounds a week. People can't do that now. And you have to be in London. I tell everyone who wants to be a critic now: somehow survive and just write, and write and write for the *Time Out*, *The Times*, any magazine. Just keep doing it!

NICHOLAS DE JONGH:

Be a theatre critic? Oh, no. If I had my time all over again, I would be a different person altogether.

ROBERT GORE-LANGTON:

Yes, I would do it again. I've enjoyed what I've been doing and when the axe falls I won't have any regrets about it. But nearly all critics' careers end in tears. In certain respects it's a thankless job because critics are all misfits, they do what they do because they love it, they don't really have any game plan, and there's no career structure – you're hired and you're fired. Then the best thing is to go away and do something else. I hope that when that happens to me I'd go and run a rather exclusive, very well-stocked bar, probably on the Cornish coast.

IAN HERBERT:

I hope I'd have the courage to force my way into a job as a director. I'm still not really convinced that theatre criticism at the level most of us practise it is a suitable job for a grown-up.

ROBERT HEWISON:

In an ideal world it wouldn't be necessary for me to be a theatre critic. I'd make sufficient money from writing books which involves theatre criticism as well, because the theatre is central to contemporary cultural history. Unfortunately an ideal world doesn't exist.

JEREMY KINGSTON:

Yes, of course! Please!

ALASTAIR MACAULAY:

Yes, I love it. It's a constant education, and it reconciles my heart and my head – makes me think about what I feel. It enriched my spirit, and opened my mind. On the other hand, I've had this life, haven't I? If you gave me a new life to live, then I might do something different. I'd be an actor, or a dancer, or a singer. Or a woman. Or a farmer. Something I have not done in this life. Another way of experiencing the world.

SHERIDAN MORLEY:

Oh, yes! I don't understand the rest of life, I understand plays. Because I come from a family of actors and directors, and I do work as a director and as show-host, I know what makes a play work. But just to be a critic is not really enough. Critics should not just go to the first night as if they had come off Mars. I like the idea of critics understanding the process. They should go to rehearsals, do some acting themselves and also get reviewed. It's very important that people who write reviews should receive them. I've written 20 books and I've had everything – from great reviews to really suicidal reviews. There are two things that an actor must never be able to say to a critic: "You don't know what it's like to be reviewed!"and "You don't know what it feels like on stage." I'm not sure whether the critic should write books or plays or do a show, but he must have this experience.

DAVID NATHAN:

Oh, yes, I would become a critic again. I've had a great time. But again I would become not only a theatre critic, but a writer on the arts and entertainment in general. I covered the Venice, Berlin and Cannes film festivals for many years and have travelled all over the world meeting people I would never have had the chance to meet otherwise. I've also written six books, two radio and one television play. This has allowed me to share in the co-operative effort that is behind every production. The experiences have been invaluable.

BENEDICT NIGHTINGALE:

I might do it in a slightly different way, but I think I would.

IAN SHUTTLEWORTH:

I'd absolutely do it all over again and do it earlier.

CHARLES SPENCER:

I love it and I'm happy in my work but I'd like to do something socially more useful. I'd rather be a doctor or something like that. I've also written a couple of novels and I felt a big need to do that. It's making something up rather than describing what someone else has done. The first book got some good reviews but the first reviews that came out were hostile. I felt blind rage, sickness and fury, and I suddenly realized how hurtful words could be and what people must feel when they read reviews. It was a very helpful experience. The other thing I realized is that even in the good reviews all you want is unqualified praise. I thought what quotes could be used on the back of the paperback. You don't give a toss about whether reviews are well written or illuminating.

IRVING WARDLE:

Yes, I would become a critic again. I've been fantastically lucky. My life coincided with the period when theatre was doing extraordinary things. I've met a lot of people I'm fond of. I don't feel I'm a frustrated artist. I can write criticism quite well sometimes, as well as most of the people on the job. I haven't got tired and I've come out at the other end not feeling an old chap yet.

Part II
Is The Ideal Really That Ideal?

1

BRITISH THEATRE CRITICISM – VIRTUES AND VICES: CRITICS REVIEW THEMSELVES

Paul Allen
Kate Bassett
Michael Billington
James Christopher
Michael Coveney
Nicholas de Jongh
Jane Edwards
John Elsom
Lyn Gardner
Robert Gore-Langton

Bill Hagerty
Ian Herbert
Robert Hewison
Alastair Macaulay
David Nathan
John Peter
Ian Shuttleworth
Charles Spencer
Jack Tinker
Irving Wardle

They answer the questions:

– What are the main strengths and weaknesses of the current British theatre criticism? Are there any special problems it faces today?

PAUL ALLEN:

It has the strengths and the weaknesses of the kind of theatre we have. At its best English criticism does much the same as English acting does, which is psychological truth to the moment. We are best at describing what we've seen and what we've felt there and then. To move on to an analysis of it is quite difficult. We are sometimes slow because we have very little theory. We can see the surface trends which affect the market and we can see the style of surface things but we're not very good at spotting the underlying shifts. Sometimes we are altogether too flippant about ideas and too insular about our theatre. We have very little theatre from abroad here and we have very few critics who are good at dealing with it. We have the Western media's appalling gift of building somebody up with enormous excitement and then destroying them very quickly. So the hardest thing for a new playwright is to write his second play.

KATE BASSETT:

One strength is that it's simply very readable. Some continental criticism sometimes seems weighed down with academic jargon. I like British critics' colloquial style combined with intelligent incisiveness. Another strength is that most of the main critics are informed and seriously interested in the theatre while being independent of the theatre business. As for problems, reviews seem to be given less and less space because allegedly reviews don't 'sell' papers. The pushiness of the PR business these days is also probably encouraging unjudgemental 'puffs' (pre-show features) rather than critical assessment. Maybe it's all part of the 'dumbing down' of culture. There's a tricky problem too – an on-going one – about how separate the critics and the theatre practitioners should be. You can't be bosom buddies. On the other hand, critics are sometimes ill-informed about how companies are working, what the state of the arts is, because there is too little communication between the two sides.

Other problems? Theatre fatigue. Seeing so much theatre your soul glazes over. Going to the theatre is damned anti-social too as a daily job, especially if your friends aren't all theatre-fans or have small children. You know, "Are you free on Monday night? No. Tuesday night? No, right. Wednesday? Erm ... " Luckily, I have very patient friends.

MICHAEL BILLINGTON:

Its inherent shortcomings are mainly to do with the speed of judgement. That's a result of the journalistic conditions under which we write. Deadline and space pressure explains a lot: if you've only got 60 minutes, or sometimes even 40 minutes, to make up your mind, there's no time to think. You simply have to express a reaction very quickly. That leads to overpraise, excessive abuse or superficiality. Someone said that no play is ever quite as good or quite as bad as it appears on the first night. That's profoundly true and if you rush out of the theatre either in a state of excitement or in a state of despair and go to your word-processor, you tend to overblow your reactions. The history of British post-war criticism is littered with examples. *Waiting for Godot*, *Look Back in Anger*, Edward Bond's *Saved* – all these key-plays were ridiculously received by overnight critics. But I can understand the reasons why. What happened was that on Sunday nearly all those plays were reassessed much more sympathetically. There is a very interesting more recent example – *Blasted* by Sarah Kane. It produced extraordinary reviews: moral outrage, intemperate disgust, shock. I'm ashamed of my own review now. A day or two of contemplation would have led us to realize that the dramatist was overloading the play, but that it made a very serious moral point.

The strengths of British criticism are a kind of ecclecticism and openness to a lot of different forms of theatre because we are exposed to a very wide variety of theatre. In Europe there are very fine critics but they see a much narrower band of theatre because there's little commercial theatre outside the subsidized section. The other strength of the British critics is that we are all journalists rather than academics. I'm not being rude about academics but collectively we have the ability to know how to address the reader and not get weighed down by theory. In France or Germany the critics are much more theoretically inclined than we are. We are much more pragmatic.

JAMES CHRISTOPHER:

The strength is that there is no one newspaper that dominates the whole scene and the writing is interesting because the critics are so different. There's also less of a sense of an agenda about writing, which is a difficult thing to achieve. A weakness is that a lot of critics can be too academic. Sometimes that's appropriate – if you want to give a sense of perspective to the development of a particular play. But in terms of reviewing, it is often a self-indulgence that pumps up the importance of the critic. It's actually doing a piece of theatre history rather than reviewing a production. Another danger is losing perspective. You can see it happening to a lot of critics. They've seen too many shows and their views have calcified and hardened. They are no longer open to new experiences. After a certain number of years critics should be forced to take a sabbatical or step aside because they lose their perspective.

MICHAEL COVENEY:

British criticism's main strength is its decency. There's no vanity involved. People do it because they love the theatre. The thing that's improved in the past ten years is that there's a curiosity about international theatre and that's thanks to people like Michael Billington and Michael Ratcliffe. When I was working on *Plays and Players* in the '70s, I used to be invited to festivals like BITEF Festival in Belgrade and this for me was a formative thing. The first time I saw the Taganka Theatre of Lyubimov was there. I was young and this had a great influence on me. I saw the Rustaveli Theatre by chance. I was the first Western critic to see them, wrote about them, and the Edinburgh festival director John Drummond invited them and they were a huge success ... The coverage of the regional theatre has changed in my working lifetime too: it's much more widespread and generous.

A weakness is that we're still trapped into writing about The National Theatre and RSC. They do about 25 new productions a year, so half of the time you're writing about them. Then, we're still too slavishly concerned about reviewing all the West End openings. We are too nervous to just say "No" to commercial theatre and go to where it emerges. We have to strike a balance. A problem that we all face is that many people in the newspapers don't think that theatre is very important. One of the ironies of new technology was that it brought forward the deadlines and most of the papers stopped doing overnight notices. The effect is that less plays are covered, that theatre is not any more treated as news, and that the critic is pushed aside.

I'm surprised that many people think that the end of the overnight reviewing leads to better criticism. I don't think so. I disagree with Michael Billington who thinks he needs more time. He doesn't. He is fantastic when he writes – bang! – like that. He's very good always when he writes next day. Otherwise criticism loses its heat.

As the information revolution continues there's more features and previews, there's more information about the same narrow number of things, and the great opportunity that the critic has is to stand out against it and be an abrasion against that tendency.

NICHOLAS DE JONGH:

I wouldn't want to get into any situation in which I criticize my colleagues at all. Generally speaking the majority of theatre critics in London write very well indeed. The writing is clear, eloquent, and vividly conveys the sense of theatrical productions. The criticism is practical as well. The failure relates to writing about stage design. There's perhaps a tendency for a few critics, who read English or History at university, to treat plays as texts – they are happy to see an unadorned stage, a production without decor.

JANE EDWARDS:

Most of the critics do have a passion for the theatre and a number of them write very elegantly and eloquently. The strengths and the weaknesses are entangled really. The main problem is that most critics have an English

Literature background and they can treat theatre as literature. They look for the themes in a new play, quite rightly, but don't give you a feeling of what it was like to be there, why one actor was better than another and what the production looked like. That can be the hardest thing to do. That's why a wonderful festival like the London International Festival of Theatre (LIFT) is ignored by too many of the number-one critics. I wish there was also a broader spectrum of people writing about theatre but only if they have something interesting to say.

JOHN ELSOM:

British theatre criticism lacks intellectual depth. We need to encourage a sense of moral indignation. I don't mean a facile moralizing. There is so much underneath the defensive, ironic liberalism: the sloppiness, the tendentiousness, the prejudices, the false political correctness. Why have we been very favourable to certain women writers? Simply because there are too few women writers, so you start to overpraise them, whereas they are actually not very good. It doesn't work if you're trying to convince an audience when the play isn't any good. We live in a world where theatre people tend to be naive and critics tend to foster that naivety, which is dangerous. The negative thing about it is that people are copping out, avoiding big issues, praising and blaming with no sense of convictions.

But I don't find this in the work of the critics I like. I like the work of Irving Wardle, Benedict Nightingale and Paul Taylor. The good thing about our criticism is that there are still a lot of people who can write well, clearly, and with an awareness of the reader and the theatre.

LYN GARDNER:

The main strengths are the sheer number of publications, the diversity and the number of critics. Women are still extremely under-represented. Some of the weaknesses are that the West End is given weight over other kinds of theatre. Most critics see very little beyond the mainstream. There are whole areas of theatre – ethnic theatre, visual theatre, physical theatre – that still get very little attention. I still think that many critics have failed to develop the vocabulary to deal with work which is visual and because it makes them uneasy they avoid engaging with it. But to really cover those areas of work you would have to completely change your agenda and the newspapers are very reluctant to do so. Another weakness is that we overpraise enormously. Sometimes we are cheer-leaders. You look at the *London Theatre Record* and you read things like "Brilliant!", "Marvellous!" when it actually was pretty average. I'm as guilty as everyone.

As for the women critics, it's really very hard to be a critic and have children. I have a five-year-old and a baby and I'm away a lot. I very seldom put them to bed. You do pay a price. It's one of the reasons so many women give it up, and once you stop there is no coming back. There are too many bright, ambitious young minds coming up behind you.

ROBERT GORE-LANGTON:

The lack of space in the newspapers is a big problem. It's a disaster that so much space on arts pages is given over to pop-music which is to be dealt with elsewhere. Film and rock have replaced theatre in editors' minds. Theatre is considered elitist, a bit of an irrelevance. Another problem is that the critics are far from being too tough on what they see, which is what a lot people in the theatre community think. They're actually too nice about things. We're all guilty of that. We're all too nice about second-rate work and most deservedly unfinished work that shows promise. We all dive on new plays that are half good and we battle up the writer's career by telling them that they're wonderful too early on.

As for the strengths, there's a community of critics here and there are many good ones. A lot of critics do it not as a career move to some other job but they do it because they love it, and enthusiasm is probably the key to the best theatre criticism.

BILL HAGERTY:

The strengths are in the numbers of very good people writing criticism. A weakness is that a lot of theatre criticism is still very pretentious. It's hard to understand it sometimes. I don't think it's showing off. I think people actually believe this is the way to approach it and yet you find that their work is so obscure that not only you have got very little idea what the play or show is about, but you don't really care. You can't be bothered to get to the end of that kind of criticism. There are not many of them but some critics write themselves into blind alleys, becoming terribly obscure.

IAN HERBERT:

The strengths come from the fact that we have so much theatre, so you don't get into the habit of reporting again and again on the National Theatre's latest staging of its latest version of, say, Molière. There's a wealth of productions to compare, and a good number of people doing the comparing.

Weaknesses? Our critics are clever, talented and perceptive, but they can be rather vain. I am suspicious of a critic with too great a sense of his own importance. The people who are really important in the theatre are the actors, the directors, the writers ...

Problems? There is a generational change going on in theatre at the moment but less so among the critics. We have a core group of considerable ability and knowledge, who have grown up with the theatre of the '50s and the '60s as their model, and their response to the new theatre of the '90s is crucial. It may be that someone who's been writing criticism for 40 years isn't going to be ready for the violently new kinds of theatre we are seeing, which attack what the older generation have developed as their idea of the perfect play. Of course, most of the critics are able to adapt to the new forms – people like Michael Coveney who knows the European theatre well and is still open to new styles, while not being afraid to point out those new theatrical emperors who have no clothes. Michael Billington, too, looks beyond his own doorstep.

ROBERT HEWISON:

The strengths are: it's lively, rigorous, many-voiced, actively engaged, it has a lot of outlets and, although its job is not to support the theatre, it's related to the ideal of a living theatre. Some of my colleagues are definitely driven by their passion for the theatre, which is admirable. I admire their commitment.

A weakness is that it's aesthetically virtually blind. Because people spend their lives in the theatre, they don't read enough books, don't go to enough films, don't see enough works of visual art ... It's also anti-intellectual. For the most part critics are conservative. In that respect they are reflecting British culture which is anti-intellectual, and apolitical. But there's a second generation of critics beginning to emerge now – people who started writing for the fringe or the alternative newspapers, people who have spent a lot of their apprenticeship writing about fringe shows.

Another problem is that we are curiously homogeneous in our social background: all white, male, middle class, university educated. Some are heterosexual, some are not, but there are very few women critics, and there are very few critics who come from other than a narrow social and cultural formation. But, on the other hand, being a critic is a very anti-social existence: people have to work every night as opposed to working every day and they don't necessarily have the best of lives.

ALASTAIR MACAULAY:

There are two most obvious things that alarm me about British theatre criticism. Actually, both here and in America, too many critics are not brave enough to attack shows that are probably successful in audience terms. He's a brave critic who will carry on saying *Les Miserables* is a bad show, now that it has been an audience success for 12 or more years. Secretly, few critics really like *Les Miserables* at all, but now everybody starts to express a certain respect for it because it is still popular. And it still is a terrible show! You can't seriously admire Shakespeare and like *Les Miserables*. The one makes you intensely more human, the other intensely less human. A lot of critics do have variable sets of criteria whereas true criticism, I'm afraid, involves rigour.

Another problem comes from a kind of déjà vu boredom which is a very great danger for English theatre critics. In England because we see so much of certain classics, especially Shakespeare, people too often are looking not for the good *Hamlet* but for the different *Hamlet*. They have lost interest in *Hamlet* itself. They also want something that will make exciting reviews. Therefore they develop a decadent form of criticism, where the classics are addressed in terms of what is most sensationalist about their latest productions, rather than what is serious. Certain traditional but good values in theatre are being neglected in this pursuit of the new and the sensational.

As for the good things about our criticism, there's still a lot of simply good writing in Britain. The average British theatre critic can command a handsome, elegant, witty sentence. He or she is also usually well-informed about a wide range of theatre. It's not just *Hamlet*, most of us have normally seen *Titus Andronicus* at least twice. In most other cities, most theatre critics have not yet seen *Titus Andronicus*. Or *Punishment Without Revenge*. Or *The Liar*. Or *Figaro Gets Divorced*. We also have more good new plays generally than probably anywhere else in the world. Our new plays perhaps deserve more severe criticism than my colleagues are giving them, but nonetheless the level is not bad.

DAVID NATHAN:

The main strengths are the variety of opinions and the general high standard of writing. I'm sometimes deeply impressed by the way my colleagues express themselves. The downside is that we sometimes get pompous and carry our prejudices into the theatre. We need to be open all the time. I know it's very difficult. If I have a firm belief which I've held for 30 years and I see a play which cuts into it, it's very likely that I'm going to resist it. But I shouldn't.

JOHN PETER:

Unlike a lot of critics on the European continent, we are very aware of the needs of the reader. We tend to avoid elaborate technical terms, explanations, and theorizing. British readers tend to be apprehensive about anything serious being said about anything they enjoy. Sometimes we may even go a little too far in the other direction. The British reader likes to be cheered up so we cheer him up. The best example of this is the attitude to humour in serious theatre. We want to tell our readers that it's not all unrelieved gloom, that it has laughter in it too. We sometimes tend to soften the blow because we know deep down that British audiences are sometimes unconsciously reluctant to go and see anything that's going to upset them.

The great strength of British criticism is a practical outlook on how the thing is actually done. We tend not to be too reverential, whereas in the continental countries criticism has an aspect of built-in hero-worship. There are actors and directors who are barely criticized except in the most oblique way. British critics are more relaxed, less inhibited and have fewer pre-conceptions. We might say, "Look, this is a great play but the last speech is twice as long as it should be." British critics don't like being driven by concepts. They are more open, matter-of-fact and outspoken.

IAN SHUTTLEWORTH:

The major weakness is that British criticism's place in the media has been marginalized. Its strength is that it continues to draw intelligent people to it despite the smaller role that it's assumed to have. Another strength is the plurality of theatre voices: there's always a healthy disagreement and a healthy debate. There are a number of younger critics coming up who are beginning to break the current mould of British theatre criticism as always being conducted by white, middle aged, middle class men. It's not a major revolution but at last, little by little, things are beginning to move: more women, more non-anglosaxon critics are coming in. Another thing that's in a process of change is the unwritten rule that critics won't discuss a show before they've been in print about it. That applies less to critics who are friends. It also applies less to my generation. We have fewer reservations about getting into a heated debate in the bars after the show

CHARLES SPENCER:

I don't think we've got a great critic at the moment. There isn't someone of the stature of Ken Tynan and we need someone like that. It would possibly raise all our standards because we would all be in competition with him. The good thing is that because there are so many of us working on national papers, no one person has the killer punch. If we've got a fault, it's that we're far too kind. We tend to say that things are very good when they're good, that they're good when they're fair, and that they're fair when they're poor.

JACK TINKER:

I don't think we have any critic who, like Tynan, could make theatre live on the page. You read Tynan's reviews and you can see the play. But as a collection of individuals the critical body in England is an extraordinary cross-section of opinion, prejudice, and enlightenment. That's very healthy because that's what our audience is like.

IRVING WARDLE:

The danger criticism faces is that the newspaper editors think that public can do without it and that anyone can criticize. One of the weaknesses of criticism itself is that it's quite rare now to find really good descriptions of acting. The critics who were writing when I was a boy were quite good at describing. You'd look at their columns and you'd get quite clear critical accounts of performances. This is one of the central lines of British criticism going to Tynan. It was the actors who rescued the English theatre from the grip of Aristotle. And reviewers were part of that process. They've repaid the debt, paying an awful lot of attention to actors ever since. But we aren't doing that to the same extent now.

Reviewing is improved now in terms of comparing what's on the stage with what's in society outside. The negative thing about that is that most of the reviewers are not really political people. They tend to get their political and social vocation from the theatre. Rather than actually having read Marx, for example, they get the idea of Marx from what David Hare writes and then they try to draw conclusions about society at large. This is just the wrong way round. The only one who really does know about politics from personal experience is John Peter on *The Sunday Times*. I respect him a lot. The other negative thing is that a lot of us review themes instead of plays. If the play has an important theme, it gets marked up, even though it may be not well written. Plays about something utterly insignificant, like somebody having a love affair, get marked down, even though they may be well written. This is ludicrous!

A strength is that there isn't so much malice here. We don't have anybody like New York's John Simon. People write with good faith and try to tell the truth. A lot of them have insights into how plays are put together. They're good at analysing. But there is a feeling of a car with the wheels turning around not really in contact with the road because we're going through a pretty dull period.

2

CHANGE OF THE ROLES: THEATRE-MAKERS CRITICIZE THEIR CRITICS

Playwrights:

Steven Berkoff
Arnold Wesker

Directors:

Howard Davies
Sir Richard Eyre
David Farr
Jonathan Kent
Nicolas Kent
Sam Mendes
Katie Mitchell
Trevor Nunn
Adrian Noble
Max Stafford-Clark

Producers:

Thelma Holt
Sir Cameron Mackintosh
Michael Morris
Tom Morris
Peter Wilkins

Press-Agents:

Martin Coveney
Sue Hyman
Sharon Kean
Sue Rolfe
Joy Sapieka

They answer the questions:

– What are the main strengths and weaknesses of the current British theatre criticism? Are there any special problems it faces today?

STEVEN BERKOFF:

Generally there is a higher standard of criticism in London than in New York because there are many more papers. There are very good reviewers here but there are no brave ones writing at the moment. A really receptive one is Robert Hewison at *The Sunday Times*. He is the most interesting and his culture goes through many different avenues, particularly visual arts. I don't demand a good review from him but usually he is honest, perceptive and makes you proud. Unfortunately the *The Sunday Times* main critic John Peter makes sure Robert Hewison doesn't review me. Peter's enthusiasm for the theatre is unconventional but he has a kind of wilfulness to abuse, to beat. His reviews for me have been the worst. I also suspect him of contributing to the erosion of 20th-century theatre in this country. The person is probably a very pleasant man and occasionally has given me a moderately good review for my acting. In fact he even praised my last play's 'message'. But he does not understand – the same way you can't read shorthand. However if you don't understand it, you don't read it. But some other critics do a very good job. Jack Tinker was a fair critic. There was a great enthusiasm in his writing. Nick de Jongh hasn't always been a fan of mine but there's an element of enthusiasm in his writing as well. When he writes, you want to read him. Irving Wardle has always been a fair person and writes with insights. I was very flattered by Nick Curtis of *The Evening Standard* in a review of *Coriolanus*. I don't just like them because they like me and I don't hate them because they hate me. If they disliked me but they were fair, I would accept it. But if they're unfair, that's bad.

The weakness of much of the British theatre criticism is its parochialism: it's too dull in its tastes, it's too British-bound. Because of the English language and the way it's spoken everywhere, critics are lazy about investigating other theatrical corners. Nothing much happens in English language any more. Most things are happening in other languages, in other theatres, in other forms. Another problem is the space for criticism in the papers. At *The Times* the art section is two pages whereas the sports section is 10 pages. Ten! I counted them one day just for the sake of it. There should be 8 pages for the arts and you don't want any pages on sports. Who's obsessed with sports? People who like sports are not obsessed. They are interested in it. But people interested in the arts are obsessed. They want to see what's going on, they follow it, they study it for years.

MARTIN COVENEY:

The main strength of the British criticism is its diversity.

HOWARD DAVIES:

The advantages are that there are so many different voices here unlike New York. To a certain extent it allows the critics to be their own person.

SIR RICHARD EYRE:

We are quite lucky: we've got a number of people who write well and passionately about the theatre. It's probably a bit too much of a closed circle. It's up to the editors to try to inject new blood into this system. But I think it's difficult because there are very few people who want to write criticism . . . We have many newspapers, so it makes a sort of consensus. That's one of its virtues. But the newspapers should give more space to the theatre, so that the critics can write in much further detail.

DAVID FARR:

There's a great enthusiasm for the diversity of theatre. There's a tremendous support for the smaller theatres. A lot of European classics or playwrights, who were seen as very difficult and impossible 10–15 years ago, have now become a part of the euphoria of the whole theatrical system. That was started in small theatres like the Gate and the critical process has been very strong in picking up on that. There are several critics – Michael Billington, Michael Coveney, John Peter, and Irving Wardle – who are particularly enthusiastic about opening up the British view of the theatre world. What is less clear is the agenda of the younger critics. The older critics instinctively see theatre as central to our culture. The younger critics won't talk about theatre as a serious art medium. They question it all the time. Theatre criticism needs to address very quickly this problem. One occasionally reads an article by an old critic who says why isn't it as important as it used to be in their day. And then one would read young critics who are simply not addressing this problem but getting around it by simply attacking individual productions for not being modern, or using strange terms that may not necessarily apply to the form.

There is a strong Shakespearean critical process which I find negative in terms of its introspection: it's impossible now to produce one Shakespeare production without it being referred constantly to others. That seems to me to be a downwards model.

THELMA HOLT:

The main strength is the quality of writing of our critics. They are generally very well informed and informative. They are usually also well educated theatrically. Many of them travel overseas a great deal, and they all see an enormous amount of theatre. Michael Coveney, for instance, discovered the Rustaveli Theatre Company in Tbilisi, Georgia. He subsequently introduced me to their work. This is not unusual with critics in this country, and I would imagine is also the case elsewhere.

The first big international season at The Royal National Theatre in 1987 had huge support from the Critics Circle. They all gave advice as to what should and what should not be presented before our audience. This sounds a bit like a hymn in praise of critics. There are, of course, the negative sides, but these aspects I usually ascribe to the writers I do not regard as critics: they have the job by accident, and hopefully will not last too long in it. It irritates me that there are those who do not understand that a piece of theatre is a living thing and when you see it on stage that is not the end. It will keep changing and hopefully growing. Few pieces of work are perfect: they do not need to be. It is a world that attracts a new audience, and there is a sense of danger. There are critics who have fallen into it and would in truth prefer to be acting, directing, or writing plays. I think that is disastrous. As with all branches of this profession, to do it properly, you need to be totally committed, and the critics need to be as passionate about their jobs as the artists themselves are.

SUE HYMAN:

Reviews are probably too obscure. They aren't comprehensible to normal readers. Critics are sort of writers for Oxford academics.

SHARON KEAN:

One of the problems, particularly with revivals, is that the critics have seen the play a number of times before and therefore they are not coming to it fresh. Criticism then can become a comparison between the productions they've seen two, five, or 20 years ago and the new one. Whereas the people they are writing for sometimes haven't seen any previous production and the comparisons don't mean anything for them.

When we've done projects with American critics involved, it seems to be a more sycophantic and demanding relationship there than it's here. British critics don't seem to prove that demanding. I find British criticism much more straightforward. That makes it very difficult for us, the PRs, because a terrible review could be at the same time very funny. Michael Coveney, for instance, has written the funniest reviews I have ever read.

JONATHAN KENT:

The strength of British theatre criticism is that there are an awful lot of critics, so you get a cross-section of widely different tastes and you don't have to rely on the opinion of one man as in New York. The dangers are that newspapers are going helter-skelter for a sort of populist appeal. There's a fear of taking art seriously. Somehow it has been trivialized. Arts journalism has been caught up in a sort of sensationalism and even good criticism is being diminished. It is particularly noticeable in *The Guardian* which, until recently, appeared to take the arts seriously, but it is happening in many newspapers. I don't know what their policy is any more. In addition, criticism is slightly fossilized: a lot of the critics have been doing it for an awfully long time. We need a new energy, a new drive.

NICOLAS KENT:

The strength is the diversity of critics' voices because of the number of newspapers published here. A strength used to be that reviews came out the next morning, so it had a sense of occasion, it was news. It's no longer news now.

A weakness is that criticism isn't rigorous enough, it tends to be too kind to everything. It's become bland. There are one or two young critics who bash everything but there's no one in between who's in love with the idea of going out for the evening and celebrating theatre and trying to find its communication with real life.

The main problem is that British criticism has become a hothouse: many critics are not living in the real world. They don't live in Kilburn, they don't understand what we're trying to do within our multiracial community, and they are not writing for our community. They are cultural cowboys: they come in and collect a play, and they are not looking at it in a context. I don't mean they should be sympathetic to the theatre. They might dislike what different theatres are doing but they should at least understand what they are trying to do. I would love theatre criticism not to be a profession but rather to be undertaken by writers who write about music, cinema, do a bit of reporting, or are even novelists or historians. Critics are all white, middle-aged and male. We have never seen a black reviewer here. Hardly ever have we had a woman reviewer. It's ridiculous because our audience is predominantly women and it's often at least 40% black. Also they are often setting one performance against something else that they've seen elsewhere and most of their audiences don't necessarily share that understanding. I also have some difficulty with the fact that most of the critics in this country have been critics for so long that they have become rather jaded. Nothing is new for them and they don't have any sense of excitement. They see other critics in the interval, they influence each other, they react off each other, and it becomes very incestuous.

SIR CAMERON MACKINTOSH:

We are lucky in this country that we have so many newspapers that write about the theatre and the majority of the critics have devoted their lives to their profession. Therefore there is a very good chance that some of them will reflect what the general public thinks. That's the major strength. The downside is when they get on a high horse about what the theatre should be. I think a healthy theatre totally depends on healthy new writing. Many of the current crop of critics are showing an alarming tendency to yearn for musicals in the traditional Broadway Musical Comedy style rather than being able to appreciate new writing. But this kind of show, however enjoyable, is not the future. Producers, directors and critics shouldn't try and make people write in a particular way. It's only when writing in the theatre is surprising and different, that we get something exciting. The other thing that the critic needs to be aware of is that real talent is very rare and when it's there, it needs to be nurtured. Therefore, they should think twice before they hatchet the career of somebody who may end up one day writing a classic, but could be easily destroyed just for a quick laugh. Usually writers survive. Stephen Sondheim's scores are often underappreciated by the critics and the score of *Les Miserables* was mostly dumped on when first heard.

Another problem for the commercial theatre is that there are critics who give such incredible reviews for something done on the fringe which is then transferred to the West End where the general public doesn't like it because the show wasn't conceived for a major auditorium. They need to be careful about seeing things for what they are and not making generalizations like, "This is the greatest musical in London!" or "This is the best play London has ever seen!", when they are only in the back-room of a pub.

Another problem is that since a lot of the British critics are brought up on the classical dramatic theatre, they find it difficult to take serious musicals seriously. They can react to fluffy musicals like *Crazy for You* and *42nd Street*, and embrace them because they are more comfortable with the tradition of the Broadway musical that they were brought up on. Whereas the American critics consider all musical theatre seriously and therefore they look at even the fluffiest musicals seriously. If you look at the reviews for *Les Miserables* in America, they saw nothing wrong in a serious work being the basis for a musical. Over here the majority of critics reviewed the idea of taking a classic book like *Les Miserables* and making it into a musical. The reaction was: how dare he musicalize it, and how dare it be done at the RSC?

SAM MENDES:

There's a misunderstanding of the difference between opinion and criticism. Opinion is saying, "This is the best production I've ever seen," and not explaining why. I'm not interested in what a critic thinks is the best or worst, if they can't express why. If you are only relaying the plot, or showing off your knowledge of how many productions of the same play you have seen, and you can't communicate the excitement or boredom of the experience, then you're not a critic, you are a columnist. Sometimes it's merely, "This is my judgement." That's not necessarily the critic's fault. They have less and less space to convey their thoughts. We get more space on the dailies but if you are a Sunday critic, you are allowed space for one big production and for the others you get a paragraph!

KATIE MITCHELL:

British theatre criticism has a phenomenal understanding about the historical context in which British theatre occurred. That's wonderful. There is also a general willingness to try and understand how theatre is made. We do have a bunch of very sensitive critics who allow you the right to fail or to take a sideways step and not always get there. But not all of them. Some of them even forget what you have done.

MICHAEL MORRIS:

There is a problem with overnight reviewing. Take a 7-hour show which has taken 4 years to create. How can you do justice to it by responding to it in half an hour? Sometimes I'm afraid it's true that parts of the review are written even before they see the show. So in a way the Sunday critics are in a better situation. More time and more space. Another thing I feel concerned about is that sometimes the critics aren't in tune enough with the process that leads to different sorts of productions.

TOM MORRIS:

British theatre criticism is a successful little industry. There aren't many people involved but they are skilled people and they have large numbers of readers. I don't think criticism is strong or weak. I think it's what it is. An analogy with gossip is very good. If someone is telling a whole lot of people about something and that person has a character to their voice, and people choose to listen to that character, I can't say they should be saying something different. Because that's a real relationship and I respect it. There are a lot of people who buy *The Guardian* in order to read Michael Billington. I can't say to him, "You should write something different", because then all those people might not buy *The Guardian* any more. I have no right to comment on their relationship because I'm not a part of the interaction. I can say whether what he writes will help me or not. If I'm putting something on and I don't think Michael Billington will like it or understand it, although he is a very clever man, there's no point in my trying to get him come and see it. That's why the hardest challenge for any theatre is to find where the channels of communication which reflect what we are trying to do are.

ADRIAN NOBLE:

The strengths and weaknesses of British theatre criticism are exactly the same as the strengths and weaknesses of our national press as a whole. On the whole we have a very good national press: there is a reasonable balance of broadsheets and tabloid newspapers, the newspapers represent a political variety. That is also true for theatre criticism. On the whole criticism is reasonably respected. For example, Charles Spencer of *The Daily Telegraph* is a pretty independent spirit . . . A weakness is that criticism is not getting much space.

TREVOR NUNN:

I think matters improved a lot over the last few years. The biggest complaint that professionals working in the theatre always had was that theatre criticism was in fact journalism of the most superficial kind because the writers were being asked to reach judgements only in half an hour after the performance. So either they fell victim to being sensationalist or they had to prepare their views ahead of time and then fill in the gaps. It was generally felt by the theatre people that they should require newspapers to reorganize so that there could be much more time and consideration before reviews were published. That more or less happened.

Of course, the newspapers would say that the only thing significant to the readership is the news value of a theatre product and if that is lost, then theatre reviewing has to go to a less prominent place in the newspaper. That's happened too. The arts sections are now folded in between the sports section and the business, and the appointments section. Consequently general readers won't come across theatre reviews. I regret that.

A strength is that several of the critics have witnessed generations of work. They've been writing criticism for 20, 30 years and therefore they do have a strong sense of tradition and context. They can consult their own memories. The standards that they seek to preserve relate to judgements that they have themselves made in the past. The concomitant weakness is that a lot of very experienced critics are under threat from journalists from a much more recent generation, who first of all believe it to be their duty to entertain and to be fundamentally disrespectful of the form they are writing about. There're also journalists who believe that the personality of the writer should be more prominent than the achievement of the people they are writing about. So the by-line is now accompanied by a photograph of the journalist, who tries to portray a very strong personality and maps out his territory by making it absolutely clear whom and what he rejects. And the rejection has to be very extreme, disparaging, and dismissive. It's a division that, I suppose, has a lot to do with those who feel themselves to be a part of the post-modernist approach and who feel themselves to be out of sympathy with post-modernist, nihilistic, and non-narrative views. In cinema it's almost as clearly defined as pre-Tarantino and post-Tarantino. The territory is mapped out and anybody who is outside the Tarantino approach is going to be savaged or rejected. It's a phase. I think that things of value will survive and find their reputation regardless of relatively juvenile critical dismissal.

SUE ROLFE:

The strength is that British theatre criticism has a more intellectual and balanced approach than the American type of criticism. The weaknesses are a mixture of human nature, the commercialism, and the ever-growing narrow-mindedness of the British press. Having grown up with the critics over the last 20 years, I can say that they don't tend to get better, they tend to get more entrenched and somewhat arrogant in their views. They are very bound to the national companies. They are drawn towards the obvious. Some of the best work is outside the main companies, which they just do not seek out. I don't believe this is just the editors who say that they cannot include reviews of this nature. If the critics showed the excitement of finding more original productions outside the mainstream, they'd win their case and not have to review something at The National Theatre, for example, just for the sake of it. There are not many critics nowadays who are constructively critical at all. An example would be the reviewing of productions at the Shakespeare's Globe Theatre when it opened in 1997: you could tell by the writing they were just dying to dig the knife in it. Very few journalists like to write about good news stories. And fundamentally they are journalists, not critics. If you want a more balanced form of criticism, you've got to go outside the national newspapers and look at radio arts programmes such as *Kaleidoscope* which was about the only programme left with a form of criticism which offered comparative debate.

JOY SAPIEKA:

As British culture, and therefore British theatre, are multi-ethnic, it would be a positive step if the range of reviewers reflected this. On the whole, they are still white middle-class men. They should be a much more mixed group – not only more women, but other races as well.

MAX STAFFORD-CLARK:

The situation that always arises in New York – that any play you do is immediately trivialized by the question of what *The New York Times* drama critic thinks of it – doesn't happen here. That's the main strength of British criticism. There are 9 or 10 serious critics. That means that you have to have a general consensus before you have a hit and equally you have to have a general consensus before you have a complete failure. There are at least half a dozen critics whose responses are intelligent and whose work I listen to. A weakness is that there are too many people writing from a too similar perspective. Although the critics can't help being middle-aged and male any more than I can. My criticism of the critics is that they are run by newspapers and their reviews are mainly news. So if you do a very good play that doesn't have a star in it or isn't in any way newsworthy, it's very hard to get a breadth of critical coverage and attention.

ARNOLD WESKER:

We do have intelligent critics: Michael Billington and Michael Coveney are intelligent critics. John Peter could be, if he wasn't performing all the time. Nick de Jongh is quirky and too full of spites, and not to be trusted. But with someone like Billington, and even like Coveney, you get a sense that they actually care about the theatre. If something excites them, it's a discovery. But generally I have a feeling that standards now are low and critics are more easily satisfied with spectacle rather than substance.

PETER WILKINS:

My criticism of critics is not levelled just to critics, it's to newspapers generally. The editors give very little space to openings of shows unless they are big musicals. A play only gets a small mention. It's very distressing to think that the whole of your work has been summed up in just a few inches. I don't know whether that's the fault of the arts editors or of the critics for not pushing for more space. You read *The New York Times* and there is half a page of real in-depth writing about theatre. Of course, that has its own disadvantages: you read sometimes a lengthy review and in the end you don't know whether the critic did like the show or not . . . Another problem is that nearly all the critics start from the literary side of theatre. And theatre isn't about literary work. It's about real life and human beings . . . It seems to me that our critics sometimes don't give the recognition to the skill of the actor against to, perhaps, the writing of the play. Often you see wonderful performances in a trivial play, and the play is dismissed but it might be worth paying £25 for the brilliant piece of acting.

3

ARE ALL THE BATTLES WON? (KENNETH TYNAN BEQUEATHS A CONTROVERSY)

Paul Allen
Kate Bassett
Michael Billington
Michael Coveney
Nick Curtis
Nicholas de Jongh
John Elsom
Robert Gore-Langton
John Gross

Jeremy Kingston
Alastair Macaulay
Sheridan Morley
Benedict Nightingale
John Peter
Ian Shuttleworth
Charles Spencer
Jack Tinker
Irving Wardle

They answer the question:

– Kenneth Tynan wrote to Harold Hobson: "The problem with our successors is that there is hardly anything at stake for them." Do you agree with him?

PAUL ALLEN:

There is plenty at stake if only people realize that. The real problem of the last 15 years is that questions of politics, social justice, truth and honesty have been taken off the agenda. We've lived through a period in which the only thing that was important was, "Are you a success or not?" And we, as critics, have been told often enough that it's boring to talk about moral values. But we can't go on living like that, and we are going through a period of change now. One of the ironies of that period is that there has been an explosion of playwriting by people under thirty.

KATE BASSETT:

Theatre is less front-page news now, so you might say there's less at stake. But is that actually true? In some ways they had it easier – Kenneth Tynan and co. If theatre criticism today is no longer hot news, the theatre critic is dangerously dispensable. What exactly was at stake for Kenneth Tynan? I'm not sure. If he's talking about intense commitment to theatre, I think many critics have that now too. I'm not sure Kenneth Tynan, inspiring and brilliantly eloquent though he was, wasn't prone to hype and self-hype. Exciting theatre seems to come in waves. We've just had one: a spate of immensely promising young playwrights after years when people thought the theatre was on its last legs. You do feel you have a 'cause' when talent is emerging.

MICHAEL BILLINGTON:

I don't agree. I've always been puzzled by that letter. It was written when he was very ill, quite close to death. Both Hobson and Tynan felt they were at the front line. They were there when the radical change was happening and they had to express a commitment to what was new. But Tynan's accusation is not fair because there are now other causes to fight for.

MICHAEL COVENEY:

It's true. Now it's very difficult to find what the great causes are. Tynan and Hobson had all the great battles – about the subsidized theatre, new work, foreign influence. He meant also that critics didn't write as if their life depended on that any more. I suppose we're spoiled thanks to Hobson and Tynan, and their legacy. We should thank them because they kept the debate about theatre going so vociferously and that we are their children. But although a lot of the critical writing overall is better, it's very hard to see that sort of cutting edge of criticism at the moment. That's part of the whole cultural climate. We certainly need some new young critics.

NICK CURTIS:

I have wondered, if Keneth Tynan was writing now, whether he would be able to get a job. Because there is very little space now for his type of criticism or rather for the depth of his writing. But there are still things worth championing.

NICHOLAS DE JONGH:

If Tynan means by "nothing at stake" that there are no great theatrical movements now, he's correct. We live in a society where theatre has almost been marginalized. We all pretty well agree on what constitutes good theatre. And expressionistic style of theatre production has become far more popular with audiences and actors. If he means that our jobs are not at stake – he's probably right. Most newspapers tend to keep their theatre critics forever.

JOHN ELSOM:

We are facing the basic problem of our society now: we have no system of values, no mythology, no way of sorting out our differences. What we have are the bits and pieces from mythologies of other ages but there isn't an underlying process which develops this into a more useful way of thought. People are no longer capable of standing up against things, of arguing out their cases consistently. Argument itself is at a very low ebb in British theatre. The expediency, the money grabbing, the lack of humanity was very sad in the '60s and '70s, but by the '80s you sort of got past caring. We may be approaching the end of that cynicism now. But that low point has taken a long time in coming about.

ROBERT GORE-LANGTON:

I don't agree because I think there's a lot at stake. Tynan's genius was to take theatre right into the realms of contemporary life and try to provide a blueprint for how we should live and how the theatre would be reflective in our society. Now it's a question of preserving the value of theatre as a live art because it's under a tremendous attack from all sides as an irrelevance. If it has got nothing to do with what we're all doing, then it will die. I always think when I go to a show, "Is this actually any better than watching TV?" That's the key to it. I want theatre to grow and flourish, and for people to realize that it offers more alternatives to all the visual media around. But the theatre has to earn its spurs.

JOHN GROSS:

There's plenty at stake. There's plenty to fight for. I'd like to argue about half the productions of The National Theatre and RSC, for example. I think they're distortions. I'd like to see more traditional interpretations of the classics and less political correctness. I'd like to see dramatists with a wider range of views but I can't produce them if they're not there. And I'm out of sympathy with grandiose modern musicals. I think the old light-hearted musical has been ruined.

JEREMY KINGSTON:

Recently I was reading Tynan's review of *Look Back in Anger* in which he said: "Yes, the author does go off the deep end but I don't hold that a vice in a theatre that hardly ever puts more than a toe in the water." He was trying to get people to put more than a toe in the water – to write about the issues that were around, in the language of the day of the '50s. But if he himself had been one of his own successors, he too would have had less at stake because more theatre is now coming from abroad, more things are being done than in 1956. Of course, there are still great causes to fight for. For example, I want to see every aspect of life around me in this country and abroad made stageable. I want what film can do – create worlds which can move you and yet enable you to analyse them. I want that to be possible on the stage. In the '60s I had psychotherapy that used LSD as a psycho-therapeutic tool. One of the reasons I did this was that I had been told I would re-experience my childhood and see it with my today mind, so that I could say: "I see why such-and-such happened." That's in a way how I would like theatre to be: I want to have experiences that will touch me, move me, excite me, make me laugh, and at the same time be able to work out what lies behind them.

ALASTAIR MACAULAY:

A lot is at stake. In many ways we are living in a wonderful time for going to the performing arts in Britain. But generally I do think, we are moving out of what has been a great age of world culture for the last three or four centuries, and I sometimes suspect that we are moving into the next dark age. Our cultural criteria are getting blurred in all kinds of ways. Classicism, which flourished up to Stravinsky and Balanchine, has become an endangered species. New forms of cultural Stalinism – notably, political correctness – prevail. Our sense of humanity and our sense of rhythm are getting coarse. So yes: I think culture's at stake. If you don't stick up for what you think is a part of civilization, barbarism of one form or another will creep in. Maybe it's just *Les Miserables*, but it's still barbarism. And when I look at some ironic post-modern productions, I feel the next dark age has already begun.

SHERIDAN MORLEY:

Ken proved himself into everything, and whatever he did he did it like a tornado. I think he meant that we have become more stiff or laid back, perhaps a bit too academic, we no longer display our passions on our sleeves. That's entirely true but I'm not sure it's only critics' fault. You don't find yourself passionate about nothing. And you have to crank up the passion week after week. The truth is that the easiest thing for a critic is to write about a smash hit or a real failure. The test of a good critic is: Can you write about a play which is not very good, not very bad, not very special but quite interesting in bits? Or about an actor who is not the next Olivier but not really terrible? And to make that interesting to the reader! Tynan made the top theatre brand interesting. The test now for us is to make the middle brand interesting. I don't think that we lack passion. We're just slightly more alert to the rest of the world. The theatre is no longer the only thing around – we have TV and a lot of other information coming at us. Ken and Harold Hobson managed to isolate theatre – they almost wrote in a vacuum, they hardly ever referred to the cinema and never to the TV. They treated theatre like opera is treated – as a totally self-contained, outside force. Now we are obliged to understand it in a mass-media, multi-media age. That approach leads to less electricity. Ken always talked in terms of electricity: put your finger in the plug! You can't keep doing it after a time – you either kill yourself, or the plug gets worn out.

BENEDICT NIGHTINGALE:

There's just as much at stake. You need only to open the news pages in the morning. The question is how the stage deals with what's happening now. Tynan thought that the stage necessarily had to come up with formulated answers. I think it has to ask questions.

The major challenge for any critic, at any time, is to spot talent, but much more importantly not to miss genius. The dread of any critic is that you arrive at a theatre, the posters outside saying "*King Lear*", by an unknown playwright William Shakespeare, and you've already seen three plays that week, you feel a bit tired, and you say, "Oh, God, it's going to last three and a half hours! I wish the weekend would come." But your job is actually not to miss the fact that *King Lear* is a great play and Shakespeare – a great playwright. The temptation of critics is to admire what's already been admired. To respond to the new, to see where it's just art for art's sake or showing off – that's your biggest challenge. Also, the artists themselves. The reason I left academia in America to come back to be a critic here is because I missed the actors. That's a real excitement in this country that is missing in America: to monitor the classical tradition, to be able to see major actors emerge and wrestle with the great plays and parts. One of the great challenges of our criticism is to recognize and record that adequately.

Theatre criticism is the weirdest job in the world: on Monday you review *King Lear*, on Tuesday – an avant-garde play from Holland, on Wednesday – some dopey cabaret show in the West End, and on Thursday it's a raging, angry play by some Marxist in a cellar. The same mind has to embrace all those things. Not to miss the genius among the daily grind – this is the major challenge.

JOHN PETER:

It was nostalgic of Tynan to say this. I admire him for being one of the people who transformed the face of theatre criticism. I lament the fact that he made this comment when he was no longer a critic and didn't know what the risks were. There are risks now, only Tynan gave up dealing with them after just a few years. There is a great deal at stake for me and for all my colleagues because the state of the theatre is always an indication of the state of society. The way theatre is allowed or not allowed to make public challenges to public morality and social assumptions is always a key part of life. The major things at stake now are the fate of subsidized theatre in this country and the government support for the arts. If there is no serious state support for theatre, then society loses one of its few sources of independent criticism and comment.

IAN SHUTTLEWORTH:

He's right. We know now that we can't change the world, we know that we can't even change the face of the art in that kind of revolutionary way that Tynan and Hobson helped come into effect in the '50s. And we are a lot more resigned about that. All we can do is say what we can as cogently and articulately as we can. We certainly can't sweep floors clean and erect new structures for ourselves because we are aware of that. So, yes, to that extent there is very little at stake for us. I'm reminded of Jane Austen who described her novels as exquisitely painted miniatures – maybe two square inches – in which she worked with great detail. I suppose in a lot of respects the same thing applies to the problems of the critics. We have our little areas that we can work in and write our details, but that's all we are allowed.

CHARLES SPENCER:

Tynan was always looking for the shock of the new. He probably went a bit too far on that especially in the end. I don't think *Oh, Calcutta!* was particularly worthy. No! ... You could say that most of the great battles have already been fought but there's still that moment when you come across brand-new writing and you want to persuade people that this is a night really worth witnessing. We now have a very good National Theatre and the RSC, we've got this burgeoning fringe scene. Maybe there isn't this great moment to champion someone like John Osborne as something entirely new but I bet something else will come along soon. There are still battles to be fought. There's still a lot of friction among critics – we don't all agree with each other all the time.

JACK TINKER:

Tynan was writing in a hugely exciting time and he was responsible for championing some extraordinary talent. However looking back now, I don't think John Osborne was the greatest playwright, or *Look Back in Anger* – the greatest play. It just happened to be right for its contemporary time. It's very old-fashioned now, not very well constructed and the characters are rather clumsy. But in the excitement of the time Tynan was quite right to champion it. The battle is now not about class. It is now a battle of economics – of survival of a whole class of people, of a sub-class of people. That's what young writers tend to be writing about now and there are some very exciting things coming on. There are exciting new directors. What is going on at the Royal Court now is quite the most exhilarating thing I've known for years: almost every single production that's on there is a new find or a reaffirmation of a young writer. That's because Stephen Daldry is a man with a vision and courage.

IRVING WARDLE:

In a sense Tynan was right but it was partly his own fault because he fought the battle himself. Before he won the battle, it was perfectly clear where one's sympathies lay and this engendered quite a lot of passion. Once that was over it was difficult to focus feelings with the same intensity. There isn't so much of a campaign to carry out now, it's more a question of looking at the work. Maybe this is only saying that we're back to normal. Because the main business of criticism isn't so much to fight theatrical battles but to support artists who require it and to comment on their work in such a way as to alert the public to see.

4

BRITISH AND AMERICAN THEATRE CRITICISM: A COMPARISON

Michael Billington
John Gross
Peter Hepple

Sheridan Morley
Benedict Nightingale
Matt Wolf

They answer the question:

– Could you make a comparison between the British and the American criticism?

MICHAEL BILLINGTON:

One of the things *The New York Times* has that I envy is the generosity of space. If one goes to see *Troilus and Cressida*, ideally one would like to write an essay comparing this production with the several other productions one had seen over the years. You can't do that here because there's not enough space. Also *The New York Times* publishes essays about theatre. Then: the theatre in New York has a sort of buzz. It's a crucial part of the city's life. Everyone knows about the play that's opening on Broadway – the taxi drivers, the restaurant owners – all know. There's an excitement in the air. All these things I envy. The thing I don't envy is the pressure on the critic and the economic power of the critic. In Britain one writes with relative economic freedom. I think that the American readers are more easily persuaded by critics than the British readers. The American readers read critics fervently, they wait to be told what theatres to go to, whereas here people read them sceptically or agnostically. That's the key difference.

Another difference is that in America the critic becomes a star, whereas in Britain – as someone once said on the radio – critics are middle-aged men who catch the last bus back home to Muswell Hill.

JOHN GROSS:

The most obvious difference is very banal: *The New York Times* has a virtual monopoly. Here you've got at least a dozen opinions of significance. For some plays even more. That means a variety of views. Another difference is that there's a stronger academic tradition in criticism in America: theatre and drama have a bigger role in the American universities in general than here and most American critics have at some stage taught in colleges. There you've got men like Robert Brustein who's at the university at the moment. I don't know what his equivalent would do in this country ...Again, English writing tends to be more allusive and assumes a certain knowledge to begin with Shakespeare. Critics here are not afraid to refer to productions of the past – readers would have heard of them. Whereas criticism in America is more pedagogical: everything is made clear and spelt out. But things are changing here as well: several of my colleagues complain that their editors don't let them use references without explaining them ... Another point: English journalism is more casual than American journalism in general. English writing tends to be more personal, ironical, and nuanced. Critics in America are more aware of the commercial background of the theatre. In America it's *either/or, hit or miss*, whereas here we don't want to be too extreme. Obviously this is a generalization but it's broadly true. All these differences are not unique to the theatre, they come from a general difference between the two cultures. In the American intellectual life the boundaries are very rigid: you're on this side or you're on that side.

PETER HEPPLE:

A London critic of a national paper has a considerable influence in Manchester or Glasgow or anywhere else in Britain because we are a small country. Whereas the US critics have power only in the city they work. I don't think *The New York Times* critic has any influence in Los Angeles. Presumably the critic in Minneapolis has probably got as much power in Minneapolis as the critic in New York does. I suppose that's the difference.

SHERIDAN MORLEY:

Ever since Watergate the Americans have taken journalism much too seriously. They believe that the journalists are chosen people and what they say actually matters. Whereas the English have a very great distrust of journalists. The audiences here are much more inclined to make up their own minds. They rely on their neighbours, mothers, friends, colleagues, and the newspapers are only a back–up service. There's a whole list of shows that have run despite the critics. That seems to me a very good idea because critics have the freedom to write what they believe and the audience has the right to say, "Well, we don't choose to share that opinion." Another problem of the American theatre criticism is that it all relates to New York. Also, if London can support 12 national papers, I never understood why New York could only support one. I believe that Clive Barnes is the best critic to have worked at *The New York Times*. He was vastly ahead of any of the Americans and he is still a very good critic. If I had to choose a single critic of my generation both here and in the US, I'd certainly say that John Lahr is the best critic I know. But he writes in a very different way from the rest of us: he's given 5,000 or 10,000 words, he is allowed to go anywhere in the world he wants on *The New Yorker's* budget, and most importantly he very often lives in the house of the playwright, the actor or the director before the show opens. Then his verdict takes about 10% of his review. The other 90% is what it was like to watch that show come together. Many journalists say this is not reviewing, this is a profile writing, but I believe it is reviewing.

BENEDICT NIGHTINGALE:

It's more healthy here. All 12 leading London theatre critics collectively wield less power than the one daily critic of *The York Times*. That's an astonishing situation. When I was writing a Sunday column for *The New York Times*, you'd see a preview on Saturday and the play opened on Tuesday, Frank Rich's review would appear on Wednesday, the show would close on Thursday and my review would appear on Sunday. It's much more harder to imagine that happening here. People here are much more sceptical about the critics. They depend on them less and take greater risks on going to theatres.

MATT WOLF:

British theatre criticism in general is more informed but I don't necessarily say that against American criticism. British critics have just seen more. Everyone in New York complains every spring, "Oh, there are too many shows because of the Tony awards!" The volume of work they complain about then is what we have all year round. Therefore the British critics have a better sense of context. And because Britain is in Europe, they have a broader, wider sense of history. They can be very graceful stylists, too. But the best American critics have something that even the best British critics don't: space. No one in London has the space of any of *The New York Times* critics. There are very few who have the space I have in *Variety*. My review quota can be almost 2,000 words. Another difference is the quality of penetration in the best American reviews that I sometimes don't find here. American criticism at its best is denser and less glib, whereas British criticism can be rather glib because it's written under pressure and critics sometimes are skating on the surface of the event rather than saying something substantial about it. But having so little room, how can you help but be glib? Sometimes the British critics have less than 1,000 words to review five plays. That's a shame! If I were an editor, I'd tell the critics to choose one play and say something really interesting rather than a series of witty epigrams.

Part III
Who Would Notice If The Critics Disappeared?
Disappeared?
(Theory In The Making)

1

DEFINING CRITICISM ON A FUNNY NOTE: AN EXERCISE IN SELF-IRONY

Kate Bassett
Michael Billington
Michael Coveney
Nicholas de Jongh
Robert Gore-Langton
Sheridan Morley

Benedict Nightingale
John Peter
Ian Shuttleworth
Charles Spencer
Irving Wardle

They answer the question:

– Do you have any funny definitions of theatre criticism?

KATE BASSETT:

Given the hours, I guess I'm a lady of the night. People certainly give me funny looks when I explain I'm not free in the evening.

MICHAEL BILLINGTON:

I like the one of P.G. Wodehouse. He said that you never see theatre critics in the daytime. They only go out at night like burglars up to no good.

MICHAEL COVENEY:

David Hare used to call critics "dustbin men", "refuse collectors" – we go out every night, we pick up whatever garbage is on the pavement. When Christopher Hampton was asked what he thought about critics, he said they should ask the lamp post what it feels about dogs.

NICHOLAS DE JONGH:

In some limited sense writing a theatre review is like a process of being a witness of a road accident and being required by the police to give an exact impression of what happened as soon as you can. The complexity of a road accident is amazing: two, three or five vehicles and lots of people may all be involved in a sensational process of coming together in a negative, catastrophic, but highly dramatic event. And as in the case of a road accident you have to be able to give an idea of what happened, your response to it, your analysis, your elucidation and commentary on it in the white-hot heat of the present. So I think the analogy is not altogether absurd. It's one of the reasons why it's so important to write the review overnight. Secondly, I think that a theatre critic is in a sense like a bouncer outside a night-club. Not in a literal sense but in a sense that one is considering different sorts of audiences, trying to assess or give your readers a chance of deciding whether some entertainment is suitable for them. In a vague, but not altogether impossible way, we are like bouncers. You've got to grip your readers, interest them and inform them, and this process is not necessarily the same as producing an academic or intellectual argument. We mustn't have delusions that we are diverted academics, because we're not.

ROBERT GORE-LANGTON:

Critics are people who are paid through the nose to talk out of their arses.

SHERIDAN MORLEY:

Kenneth Tynan wonderfully said that the critic is the man who knows the way but cannot drive the car. That for me is the best line.

BENEDICT NIGHTINGALE:

Being a critic is not funny actually. Sometimes it's like submitting to being run down by a car while at the same time you have to analyze the engine.

You have to make yourself open enough to let the thing take you over but there's always got to be a side of you that is alert and awake, and slightly detached – analysing and anatomizing what's going on.

JOHN PETER:

Life is funny as a whole. But for a person to make a living out of sitting in a dark theatre and scribbling down his opinions for other people to read is a pretty funny sort of activity. Then I look at professional tennis players and I wonder whether spending 15 or 25 of the most vigorous years of your life bashing a ball across a net is not even funnier. Of course, tennis players can earn millions; but I haven't come across a theatre critic yet who has made a lot of money out of being a theatre critic

IAN SHUTTLEWORTH:

When the police force was just being formed, the police didn't have any stronger powers of arrest than any of the citizens and some judge described them as uniformed members of the public. That's what the critic is: a uniformed member of the public.

CHARLES SPENCER:

I always use the one of Brendan Behan who said that theatre critics are like eunuchs in a harem: they see it done every day but they can't do it themselves.

IRVING WARDLE:

The reviewer is like a thief. The author steals from life; theatre steals from the writer making his work its own, and finally the critic steals from the theatre.

2

SERIOUSLY SPEAKING, CRITICISM IS . . . : AN INSIDERS' LOOK AT THE PROFESSION'S BASICS

Paul Allen
Kate Bassett
Michael Billington
James Christopher
Michael Coveney
Nick Curtis
Nicholas de Jongh
Jane Edwards
John Elsom
Lyn Gardner
Robert Gore-Langton
John Gross
Bill Hagerty
Peter Hepple

Ian Herbert
Robert Hewison
Jeremy Kingston
Alastair Macaulay
Sheridan Morley
David Nathan
Benedict Nightingale
John Peter
Ian Shuttleworth
Charles Spencer
Jack Tinker
Irying Wardle
Matt Wolf

They answer the question:

– What is your serious definition of criticism? What should theatre criticism be and what is it in reality?

PAUL ALLEN:

In reality we have so much theatre that it's almost like tap-water – it's there all the time. It's conceived as an essential public utility that you must have and therefore it needs an instant response, which most of the time it gets. In some ways this is good because theatre is an immediate thing and the feeling that you have when you come out of it is the most genuine one you can have. To express this feeling is one of the functions of the critic. It's also very important to theatre management that the critics' reviews give a very clear view as to whether people should go and see the play. The critics are conscious of their role in this too. Another thing that is different in Britain from theatre in other nations is that there is much greater entanglement between the London theatre and the regional theatre. The critics in theory should try to reflect this as well. But inevitably it's a different kind of an occasion if you go to Leeds, for instance, to see a play in a building which is part of the local community, from seeing a play which is put on for purely commercial purposes in London and has an audience from all over the world. This means that critics tend to live from hand to mouth intellectually: they evaluate the experience when they go there. In consequence we have very little theory of criticism just as we have surprisingly little theory of theatre. In an ideal world we'll have a complete mixture of critical approaches: we'll have critics who will respond on the night and others who will be able to set a writer in the context of the world he or she lives in, and who will be able to look at the continuities of writing and acting and the way in which people move away from these continuities.

KATE BASSETT:

I suppose we are cultural commentators. Criticism is perhaps an inaccurate name. It is description and assessment rolled into one, ideally. And I guess, it manages to be that on a good day. On a bad day, a review may be missing the point, mean-spirited, full of typos, and sub-edited by a being from Mars.

One of the most difficult things is to write about a dull mediocre show when your review has to be colourful and amusing. Sometimes you can be in danger of misrepresenting that sort of show by making it sound more lively than it is. Also in the process of writing – particularly because of the restrictions of time and space – it's almost impossible to be comprehensive and it's hard not to tilt too far into being emphatically negative or emphatically positive when part of your job is to give theatre-goers a clean sense of whether this show is worth seeing or not. What should criticism be? It should be inspiring, informative and fair – or maybe sometimes horribly funny and obviously subjective.

MICHAEL BILLINGTON:

Criticism is more than a reporting job. Ideally, if not creative, it is at least constructive in helping to nudge the theatre in a certain direction. All the role models have always been constructive critics: they've helped to shift the boundaries of theatre by writing about it. The obvious example in my lifetime is Kenneth Tynan who, when he was on *The Observer*, was not only writing about the theatre but was helping to shape it. What animates me as a critic is the ideal I have of the theatre – what it really could be. And obviously what you're doing most of the time is measuring the reality against the dream, trying to bridge the gap between what is happening and what should be happening. The fun of criticism is not talking about plays only, but talking about the culture generally – what's good and what's bad about it'. Because criticism is a social commentary as well.

JAMES CHRISTOPHER:

Criticism is an argument. You're trying to write in an entertaining way for your readers. To inform them and give them some idea of what the show is like and why the reader should or should not see it. When you are looking at a piece of theatre and you haven't picked up your pen in 25 minutes to take a note, it's either working brilliantly or it's not working at all. Checking our expectations is the routine part of the job. The most exciting theatre is when our expectations are completely taken away from us. Another important thing about criticism is that your opinion is secondary to getting a piece of theatre onto the page. The readers should get a sense of what it was there, they should get a flavor of it. If you do that work, they can read between the lines and can build their own opinion.

MICHAEL COVENEY:

In Britain theatre criticism is a part of journalism. It's a way of conducting an informed discussion about a social medium which requires a feedback. So it's a great responsibility. But doing this job is great. I can never quite believe my luck what a wonderful job I have. The harder you work at it the better it is. You have to think about the play before you go. So one's whole life is a preparation for a first night and then doing it. It's like being an athlete, you have to be trained for it. We don't all keep as fit as we should.

NICK CURTIS:

What theatre criticism should be and what it is depends partly on what you think theatre should be and what it is. It also depends to a certain extent on whom you write for, by which I don't mean any editorial interference but you have to engage the audience you are writing for. When I was younger I had a much stronger belief in theatre as being something potent, life changing, and important with a capital I. I'm now no longer convinced that it's that. I still believe theatre can be life-enhancing and at its very best it can iluminate life but that's extremely rare. Most of the time what theatre has to remember is that it's there as an entertainment form and most people are going to treat it as such. I know, for instance, that *The Evening Standard* is read by people on the tube. Therefore you don't have a lot of time to refer to certain dramatic theory or things like that. A lot of people don't appreciate that to fulfill your role as journalist you must be entertaining. I always think that my first duty is to be entertaining. My second and parallel duty is to tell the audience precisely what I think in as clear and simple way as possible. My third duty is to be honest, fair, and accurate to the theatre world, to the play I'm reviewing, or the writer or the director. Alongside that is the duty to be demanding. There is absolutely no point in critics massaging the theatre or becoming co-opted by the mentality which theatre has, that is the government isn't subsidizing us, theatres are closing, therefore critics have to go soft on us. That's just the worst thing that can happen to a critic. It's an intellectual duty that the critic has to demand absolutely the best from the theatre.

NICHOLAS DE JONGH:

The job of the theatre critic is to give a response to and an impression of a theatrical experience. Composed within your review will be an assessment of what the playwright was trying to do and how the directors and actors have brought it into life.

JANE EDWARDS:

Ideally you should give a description and a flavour of what you've seen, put it into some kind of context and deliver an opinion. In *Time Out* it's quite hard to do all that because there is so little space. In reality, you also have to write a review that is readable, that is an entertaining piece of writing. You have to please your editor or you'll be out of a job.

JOHN ELSOM:

It's a difficult job to be a theatre critic because you have to battle hard to persuade people that what you believe in is right. The death of the critic is when they become slick, when they use the same adjectives or phrases, like the same things, and lose any connection between the theatre and life. This could lead to a self-obsessed and rather masturbatory activity. Critics can too easily become narcissistic. We shouldn't be so intoxicated by our own brilliance.

LYN GARDNER:

Criticism should be exactly what the theatre should be as well: something exciting, something which makes you interested. In reality it's sort of a hit-and-miss guide, a bit like the points system of the Eurovision song contest. That is largely because good theatre criticism requires space newspaper editors don't want to give it. Theatre criticism does not lend itself to the kind of flip, ironic style that editors seem to find sexy.

ROBERT GORE-LANGTON:

It should be an account of the night that you're in the theatre. It should catch the flavor of that live experience because in a way theatre is about flavor. At its best it should be a good read. Theatre criticism that isn't readable to anyone – whether they have a knowledge of theatre or not – isn't worth it. Because in the end what theatre desperately needs is interest from people. It doesn't help if writing about the theatre is very exclusive. Criticism should take on board that there are other things happening in the world. I'm interested in the theatre from the point of view of its connection with daily life because it feeds on and it adds to what's happening in the world.

JOHN GROSS:

It depends on where you're writing for. If you are writing for a newspaper about a new play or an unknown one, you have the obligation to tell the readers what it's about. Here I feel rather an American, not all my colleagues do it. I think that you can't start making critical points unless the readers know what the subject is. Critics should spend more time on the play – its nature, literary qualities and ideas, than on the production in general. I notice that sometimes if my colleagues like a production, or if they feel they should, they take the underlying assumption of the play itself for granted. I tend to be keener on arguing about the play. I'm not a missionary but I want to encourage people to believe in the theatre and one begins with the classics and the big plays . . . One of the gifts of the critic is to be able to evoke a performance, to describe it. In the phase before there were recordings or videos, this was their most valuable task. Tynan was a more recent example – a man who could above all describe a performance, the actual physical sensation. As for the effect on those who are criticized (assuming they read you), on a deeper level criticism is a very direct transaction between human beings: you are saying something about what the other person cares most; you're dealing with praise and blame – those are very explosive things . . . The one thing that theatre people say repeatedly is that a critic should have a lot of technical experience of the theatre. I don't agree with that. I think that when they say that, they're really asking that there shouldn't be criticism, there should be simply a kind of technical reaction on the profession's own terms.

BILL HAGERTY:

To be a critic you need an awful lot of different talents. It's not just knowing the theatre very well. It's also doing it pretty fast as a journalist. Quite often the opening of a new show is the best news-story of the night, so the critic for a daily paper especially is half a news-reporter as well. It's like reporting a football match as soon as the final whistle sounds, but far more complex. Criticism should be knowledgeable but without being too erudite. Most important: it's got to be accessible. That's where Kenneth Tynan was brilliant. There are too many critics whose criticism is accessible only to people of the theatre; the readers find their reviews puzzles which need to be solved.

PETER HEPPLE:

I quite often think theatre criticism is a waste of time. Because I very often go to a production and everybody there is enjoying it, and I don't like it very much. So I think, "What are we here for after all?" Because these shows, like *Joseph's Amazing Technicolor Dreamcoat*, are going to do well regardless of what we say about them. So criticism is really quite useless when it's about a West End show. Critics are useful in going to see plays at the Bush or theatres like it. In this case criticism might bring forward a particular playwright or actor, and might even do a great deal for the personal fortune of the theatre. Wesley Shrum wrote in his book about Edinburgh *Fringe and Fortune* that critics are useful only to maintain the morale of the actors.

IAN HERBERT:

I believe very strongly in the power of theatre – as an educational, social, or political weapon. You can do the most amazing things with it. If you're a critic, you're at the leading edge of this terribly valuable means of improving the quality of life – we are commenting on whether it's being used well or not and hopefully we are encouraging the entire world to gain from the joys and the value of theatre. So the good critics are missionaries, who are desperately anxious to get others to share what they have found.

ROBERT HEWISON:

Theatre criticism is not a part of the theatre profession. It's not the job of the theatre critic to support the theatre. Quite often we're criticized for being critics. But that's our job. We are newspaper people and our primary task, as any journalist's, is to report the event. The second task is to analyze what has gone on the stage. My own particular interest, which relates to my work as a cultural historian, is to try to relate the theatre to what is going on in society at large – artistically, aesthetically and politically. Because what keeps me interested in the theatre are two things. One is the thought that what I see will never happen again, so you are witnessing a unique event in real time. The other thing is that the theatre is still the place where people come together as a community and confront, or are confronted by, issues which affect them. That's why, although I've been doing the job for 14–15 years, I'm just as interested in it as I was when I naively began in 1981.

JEREMY KINGSTON:

Good criticism should give the sight, the smell, the tension of the evening at the theatre. It should give the impression of what it was like to have been there. It goes some way to re-create the experience, insofar as this can be done by words alone. Criticism should make a judgement as to how successfully the actors, playwright, director, have achieved what the critic presumes they set out to achieve. If possible, he can place the production in the context of contemporary life.

ALASTAIR MACAULAY:

Theatre criticism is just reportage. You are simply there as a reporter, like anyone else on the newspaper. Ideally, while you are reporting, you should

also be bringing in analysis, contextualization, evaluation, and above all –
criteria. They don't have to be the right criteria for all your readers, but you
must show that you have a set of criteria. And I don't mean just aesthetic
and formal criteria, I also mean moral criteria. It's a belief in beauty, in
truth and in clarity. Some critics show all this; some don't. Some have too
cynical an attitude to show-business: if it goes over with an audience, then
they respect it. To me, that isn't enough. I know some very "effective" pieces
of theatre that stink. I'm constantly fighting the battle of the modern musical.
I think block-buster musicals really debase humanity. They present an idea
of humanity that is the most crude and cynical one available. I hate that as
a vision of people; and the fact that these shows are popular make me very
upset indeed. By contrast, I think works like *Show Boat, The Boys From
Syracuse, Annie Get Your Gun* are triumphs of the human spirit. Just listen to
what the rhythm tells you! That is one example where you should apply
moral criteria above other things.

SHERIDAN MORLEY:

We should be guides. I don't believe in the academic theories that we are
professors of drama. Although I respect a lot of my colleagues who do
believe in the academic approach. We are reporters as much as the people
who cover road crashes, the Olympics, or deaths in the family. We go along
and say what it was like to be in a certain theatre on a certain night. That is
the most useful thing we can do. Particularly with the difficulty now in
London with the bombs and with the ticket prices going up – people are
investing about a 100 pounds for two to go to the theatre with the parking
and the cost of a meal. For that kind of money readers deserve to be told
whether really they would enjoy what they would see. So if you hated it,
you must say so. But if everybody around you was cheering, you must say
that too. And the other way around. You must give them some idea of what
the reaction of the audience was. You must be much more journalistic than
professorial. That's why I like doing overnight reviews. I love the idea of
writing very fast, while the experience is still very hot.

DAVID NATHAN:

Criticism is largely conditioned by the product you are criticizing. I find
the better the play, the more it demands from the critic. Criticism should be
a guide to quality and the theatre at its best should explore and, perhaps,
clarify the dilemmas, the pain and the absurdity experienced by its audience.
That's part of it. Another part of the job is the discovery of new talent and

that's the most exhilarating thing: you come out of the theatre bursting with the joy of your discovery, and you want to tell everybody about it. On the other hand, when you see something which you believe is false, you write a review designed to keep people away. You hear all the time how hard actors work. Yes, of course, they work hard. But they don't work half as hard as the people who have to find the money to pay for their seats. They should not be cheated. There's also public taste and people will go to things you think are rubbish. This is the privilege of the pubic.

BENEDICT NIGHTINGALE:

If you write for a newspaper, even an up-market newspaper like *The Times*, your function to some extent is determined by that. They definitely want someone who is well-informed about the theatre and will keep people abreast with what's happening and what's significant. But they also want someone who's going to be some sort of a consumer guide. That is the bottom-line. Criticism ought to be an act of analysis as well. There's not much point in "I like this!" or "I hate this!", unless you rehearse the evidence. I remember setting some students in Michigan an attempt at criticism. They wrote things like, "Derek Jacobi – wow!", and I said, "Fine, that's very nice. But *why* was Jacobi good? Let's analyse it. Why did this playwright write this play and not another. What's he aiming at?" I know that's a slightly naive question. But it's a necessary question with an awful lot of post-Ibsen drama and particularly so in this country where the drama since 1956 has been having a very strong social and political content. You also have to look at each play in terms of the particular author's work: Does it represent some new departure? How does it relate to his earlier work? You have to look at it in terms of the culture as a whole – what's he adding to our culture. Then try to analyze what the director has done or hasn't done to the play. Similarly with the actors and the way the design mediates the play. Because critics are particularly weak on this area. Before you give your opinion you really have to examine all these things.

JOHN PETER:

First of all, newspaper criticism is about information. Your reader wants to know what happened last week, what plays opened where, who was in them and what they were like. That comes first. Only then do people want to know what your opinion is. In this sense the critic is a part of his newspaper's reader service. The next thing is to make your readers interested: to write well so that they'd read you. When I was on the editorial staff of *The Sunday Times*, we were about to appoint a new film critic and the editor said, "Listen, I want to appoint somebody who will make readers fight at the breakfast table on Sunday about who is going to read him first." The next thing is to be able to pass on knowledge and understanding of how plays work. I got my education partly from critics in good newspapers who could explain these things and I still think that some of Kenneth Tynan's and some of Bernard Shaw's theatre reviews are enormously enlightening about the nuts and bolts of a play. I don't believe in lecturing, but you need to be able to explain why, for instance, the Chorus in a Greek tragedy functions in the way it does. Theatre going can be exciting; there is no reason why it should not be an intelligent activity as well.

IAN SHUTTLEWORTH:

A critic is somebody who has an opinion and who ought to be able to express it forcefully, entertainingly, and with a reasonable amount of argument and back-up of the experience. Criticism is also a description of what's going on the stage. It is from the description that an opinion of the show should naturally emerge. Through the reviews we can try to encourage certain theatrical trends, and maybe to discourage others. But I don't think any theatre critic should pursue a personal agenda.

CHARLES SPENCER:

The chief function of criticism is that it should be as entertaining as possible for the reader. Theatre reviews at their best should stand up as pieces of entertainment without anyone necessarily seeing the shows. When I was a student, my father was always talking to me about the theatre, saying this play was good and that wasn't. And I'd say, "Dad, but you never go to the theatre." "Yes," he'd say, "but I read Billington on it". Otherwise, on the most basic level, we're there as reporters – to say this show took place last night and to give some idea of the plot. Beyond that, hopefully, you bring some kind of knowledge. There's so much hype now connected with the theatre that it's very important to try to sort out the good stuff from the bad stuff. I don't think theatre criticism is a great, glorious profession. There's a large element of negativity about it, which I feel uncomfortable with. Actually if you do feel too warmly towards theatre, you're going to be doing the job badly. But the thing I mostly feel uncomfortable about is that it is essentially a parasitical profession. We do feed off the theatre. We earn our living by scavenging from the theatre.

JACK TINKER:

In a populist paper the critic is the first lead that the public has to a new show. The critic is also the opening centre of an ongoing debate. The final centre of the debate is the audience. I do think that the critic's job primarily is not to give actors notes – that's the director's job. Neither is the critic's job to give the director notes – that's the producer's job. It's not to tell the producer how to do a show – that's his own job and money. The critic's job is, on behalf of the audience, to serve their newspapers with a professional opinion. The only crime that any critic can do is to be dull. It's a waste of his paper's space. He has to engage the reader first of all and put some knowledge into his review. If you call something out of tune with the drift of theatre, if you're constantly putting down vibrant new talent, first of all your public will find out and then your editor will find out.

IRVING WARDLE:

In an ideal world a critic would know everything. There would be no homework that he hadn't done. He'd have sensibility covering the entire spectrum of emotions, he'd know the entire history of the theatre, the background of all the artists. He'd be a man of untainted integrity, friendly and unprejudiced. He'd write very well; he'd make jokes, because a reviewer who's no good at jokes is like a cartoonist who can't do hands and feet. So that's the ideal. But like all ideals it's useless talking about it. In reality we're stuck with people who know a bit, who quite like the theatre, who can write a bit, who have got likes and dislikes, and who are the kind of people who don't run with the pack. One thing I'd like to put into my book about criticism, if I expand it, is the way so much of cultural life consists of being told old stories. Jan Werich, who ran the Czech Liberated Theater with George Voscovec, said, "What I resent about the political climate of this country is forcing new audiences to see an old movie under a new title. Everything that's going to happen I know it already." Reviewing is exactly the same: reviewers have favorite stories they like to tell. It's like opening a book of fairy tales. Very few come up with something fresh and from the heart. A lot of it is very routine.

MATT WOLF:

At the end of the day in reality theatre criticism is really consumer recommendation. But I'd prefer to see it as a means of continuing an unspoken dialogue between the critics and the regular readers. One of the great things about Pauline Kael, Frank Rich, and now John Lahr, is that they were always as good if not better to read after you'd seen the film or play as they were before. A critic should make readers think about something they hadn't expected or point up something surprising, or give them a fresh perspective on something they thought they understood or knew.

3

CRITICISM SHOULD BE . . . BUT IN REALITY . . . : THEATRE-MAKERS HAVE THEIR SAY

Playwrights:

Sir Alan Ayckbourn
Steven Berkoff
David Edgar
Arnold Wesker

Directors:

Howard Davies
Sir Richard Eyre
David Farr
Sir Peter Hall
Jonathan Kent
Nicolas Kent
Katie Mitchell
Adrian Noble
Trevor Nunn

Producers:

Thelma Holt
Sir Cameron Mackintosh
Michael Morris
Tom Morris
Peter Wilkins

Press-Agents and a Publisher:

Martin Coveney
Nick Hern
Sue Rolfe
Joy Sapieka

They answer the question:

– *What is your attitude towards theatre criticism? What should theatre criticism be and what is it in reality?*

SIR ALAN AYCKBOURN:

The best criticism is written by those with a genuine love for the theatre who want to convey their enthusiasm to their readers. Good criticism is always positive. Unfortunately, some critics seem not to like the theatre at all. They sustain themselves on a diet of dislike; taking a positive delight in conveying their own lack of enthusiasm to others. Those are the bad ones. The good ones don't, of course. Even at worst a decent critic manages to find something positive to say, if only for heaven's sake don't go.

For most of us, theatre criticism is a matter of finding a critic whose tastes more or less chime with your own. Beyond that though, you hope a critic will encourage you to explore areas where you might not have normally ventured.

I've never cared for critics who try to outshine the event which they're reviewing. Occasionally they entirely miss the point of some particular piece of work. Or they judge you on the basis of something completely other than they've seen the night before. Or they want to classify you, never really satisfied until they have you jammed into some tight little pigeon hole or other. But, that apart, I've nothing against critics personally. Genuinely, they have been very good to me and I've been very lucky. Someone once told me, in theatre, you either get more than you deserve or less than you deserve. I do admit I've frequently had more than I deserve.

STEVEN BERKOFF:

Criticism should be a kind of argument over the theatre activity. It should have an objectivity, a little bit of a distance and an ability to record the truth: to chart the hills, the mountains, the rivers, the good scenery and the vista of a theatre production. At the same time it might express some subjective view: how much the critic enjoyed that particular countryside. That's what I see as criticism's function. Reality is something different. There's a kind of critic who can't see and feel the terrain, and therefore can't find the way: he slips on slopes, falls into puddles, bruises himself, and curses and rages against it because he doesn't know how to deal with it. That takes a mental and aesthetic vocabulary, which is a part of education. Lacking this education will abuse the terrain. Consequently instead of saying, "This is not my terrain. I'll not choose necessarily to go there again," the critic goes on and conveys the terrain even if he doesn't care for it. What I dislike is that the critic sometimes uses criticism as a means of whipping, abuse, satirizing, and sarcasm. This is a very dangerous thing because you can sometimes be tempted towards sadism, you can abuse someone who you know cannot answer back. I've often had very good reviews but it's true that you remember the worst ones which have been disgusting and have been so inflammatory I've felt I could have sued the critics for slander . . . I would prefer a system of reviewing generally used for books. Books are not reviewed by the same critic week after week. Whereas you get one theatre critic reviewing all forms of human taste, inventiveness, culture, ideology. The suggestion is therefore that the theatre is a simplistic art form and not worthy of the same attention.

MARTIN COVENEY:

In an ideal world criticism is seeing a play you are in favour of, writing about it, and making people want to go an see it. It should be just an informed person's response to what they see.

HOWARD DAVIES:

At its best criticism should be a way of placing a play, a writer, a performance, an actor's vision, or a director's vision in a context. I find it very interesting, for example, to read Michael Billington. He has been testing his muscles regarding one thing that obsesses him: that our theatre is becoming too Americanized. He senses we are not finding our own voices and he has complained about that. He has also the honesty and the courage when he sees something like *Fool for Love* at the Donmar Warehouse to say, "Well, doing it this well I can't complain". That's good criticism. I hate when criticism is just picking up on fashionable, treating theatre as if it was a part of the gossip columns. I hate when critics start attacking only one actor, one actress, one writer, or one director, making one person responsible for something which is a communal art form. I'm not going to use critics names from over here but I know that in New York John Simon is notorious for his attacks on women simply for the way they look! It's historically dangerous and disgraceful. The same happens over here: you see reviewers just attacking somebody for their inability to fill their lazy preconceived vision of the part or play. As guardians of our theatre culture, critics at the moment are no more than reporters of an event. I wish that the editors would either give them more column inches or allow spaces for criticism by other people. At *The Observer* they used to bring in people like James Fenton, the poet, to write about theatre. That's an interesting idea. That bears a cross-over between the various art forms, rather than theatre only talking about itself, which is incestuous and dull.

DAVID EDGAR:

It's very difficult for a playwright to answer this question. A play takes between 9 months and a year to write, and it's not easy to be objective about a group of people who could destroy 12 months of your life. Broadly speaking, they are representatives of the perfect audience, they are entertainers, they are journalists, they are there to describe an event. The critics whom I value reading are the ones who exploit their greatest asset, which is that they go and see a lot of theatre. As a reader I find it very useful and interesting to read people who write comparatively. That is really valuable. With regard to how a particular individual play should be reviewed, it's good to feel that a critic is able to place a piece of work in the context of the work of that writer, director, or actor. It is exciting when you read somebody who's understood the progression in a writer's work. One accusation against the critics is that they can't distinguish between the production and the play. I personally find it quite difficult to do so. What they should do is: understand the process. There's an argument that they shouldn't go to rehearsals. But I don't think it can devalue you as a critic of frescos if you know how to paint a fresco and how it's different from painting on canvas. Possibly every few years critics should make it their business to see if the process of making theatre has changed.

SIR RICHARD EYRE:

In an ideal world any practitioner would want to hear just universal acclaim. Theatre criticism comes at you at the moment when you are most vulnerable. You have been working on a project for a very long time, you have very passionate feelings about it, you are very tired, and just the day after you have been celebrating the end of that period of work. The skin is very thin at that point. So criticism could be acutely painful. Which is why people in the theatre react so violently to adverse criticism. Months later your skin is much thicker . . . Ideally you want to read an intelligent account of what you've attempted to do and you want argument about the reasons it has or has not been achieved. You don't want someone saying, "I didn't like it. It's not for me." That's completely subjective, that's personal chemistry. When you read a well-argued review and it says, "I don't like it because of x, y and z, although at the time you rage against what the critic has said, maybe two or three months later you think, "They were right." As for what criticism actually is, there are some good critics in this country. I've been directing now for 25 years, and most of the major critics have been writing for at least that long. I know what their sensibilities are.

DAVID FARR:

There are two distinct forms of theatre criticism. One is a simple guide to what you should see. The other one is a more serious form – it's a communication between the artist and the critics, which hopefully leads to some idea of where theatre should be going. In a time when theatre is under pressure, criticism can help to salvage it as a relevant art form. Because of the increasingly small amount of room in the national papers and because of the limitations of some of the critics themselves, most of the theatre criticism in England tends to be nothing more than a notice of what the show is and whether they've liked it. Otherwise my attitude towards critics is very simple: we need good reviews to get people into our theatre, because we don't do popular stuff, so we are very grateful to the critics. It's as simple as that. It's a free advertisement if it's good.

SIR PETER HALL:

As long as there is art there will be people who react to art. So I'm not hostile to critics. There are many creative critics and there are many critical creators. There is an inevitable pressure between the critics and the person who works creatively. There has to be. But the dividing line between us is not as great as we all like to think. My feeling about critics over the last 40 years is that their general reaction is usually accurate but their analysis and diagnosis of why something is good or bad is inevitably subjective and not necessarily accurate at all. It seems to me that the most extraordinary quality of a critic is the ability to recognize completely new talent. The critic always has the horror of missing a new genius.

NICK HERN:

As a theatre-goer I'd wish that theatre criticism was utterly candid and told me exactly what the event was like, so that I don't go only to be disappointed. However, if the critics have been happy about a particular show but it's terrible, I'm even more disappointed. On the other hand, since as a publisher I've got one foot in the theatre world, I recognize the merits of constructive criticism. There's a third part of me: I know some critics quite well, and I understand their feeling that their responsibility is to their readers rather than to the theatre.

THELMA HOLT:

The critic informs his readers, and from what he has to say they decide whether they are attracted to a production. A good critic loves the theatre. I do not find it angry-making when they show displeasure with a production. It means they have been motivated by what they have seen, but they need to have a big heart as well as integrity. Critics in the league of Kenneth Tynan and Harold Hobson, no matter how much you may have disagreed with them, raised theatre criticism to an art form.

JONATHAN KENT:

Good criticism should convey to the reader an impression of what it was like to be there on that particular night. The better the criticism – the more vivid the experience the reader has. The main ability a critic should have is to convey the unique excitement of going to the theatre. It's very hard to retain this ability over years of seeing show after show.

NICOLAS KENT:

You should never judge a marriage by what happens on a wedding night but in theatre you are constantly judged by what happens on a nervous first night. The good critic should convey the excitement of the occasion and he should do it in such a way that someone who has no chance of seeing the production would somehow feel that they have been there. Critics are quite often writing for fellow-critics and for theatre people rather than writing for the audiences. The good theatre critics should be evangelizing for theatre but they don't have to be involved in the theatre profession. In a way the less they know about it – the better. They should have a strong reaction to the play not as theatre professionals but as people who are able to write well and convey what they've seen in a very good prose. Sometimes I read a critic who has captured something of the essence of a play that makes me want to see it. That is good criticism.

SIR CAMERON MACKINTOSH:

Critics should have an enthusiasm and love of the theatre as any member of the audience. Of course, no-one can be an ordinary member of the audience if you go and see over a 100 shows a year. You've got to have a screw loose somewhere to be able to manage to sit through so many productions when, however good a season is, there's always quite a lot of terrible stuff on. But I find that the critics who have remained good critics over the years are the ones who still love the theatre and still have a child-like approach to it. When critics try to review the show that they wanted to see rather than the one that the writers' wrote, then we get problems, because the critic's job is to react to a production, not to write it. If they want to see something else, they should go and do it themselves.

KATIE MITCHELL

When I first went to university, we were asked to write about the function of criticism. It was on the second day of my first year and I came to the absolute conclusion that it had no function. Now I certainly think that critics and practitioners should look for meeting grounds to ask the questions together. Because we are quite separate from each other and we satellite around each other. So my ideal scenario would be a discussion with critics to enable them to do their job to the best, and us to do our job to the best.

But since there are two types of criticism – in newspapers and in scholarly magazines, I'm in two minds about what their relationship is to us. There are people, like Richard Schechner (*TDR*), who seem to come from a much more academic way of responding to theatre: the articles are much longer and more in-depth, and you really feel you are reading a proper study of the work. Whereas journalists have a certain amount of time and they have to respond very quickly. But they have phenomenal economic power. They affect the amount of people who come and see the work, which is frightening . . .

I'd love to get critics into rehearsals. People like Michael Billington have been in rehearsals. I'd love to bring them closer to the process because they are slightly at a distance from it and therefore are not so forgiving and don't allow us the right to fail. The best critics are those who remember your last three productions and understand that the one they are watching is just a part of the sequence of work . . .

We have to be very careful with criticism particularly if it's good. Because it satisfies one's vanity, which is a force that one should be trying to annihilate. One has to keep a very pure line to one's work. That's all that matters . . .

For me my best judge is myself.

MICHAEL MORRIS:

The theatre critics are there to represent the audience. Some of them would say that they are there to serve the art form. But criticism is really journalism, reporting, and essentially newspapers have to inform the public. At best when I read a review I want to see an indication of whether or not the show is something I might want to see. I also want to see the show put in context. No performance should be seen in isolation . . . The theatre critics I respect are very subjective.

TOM MORRIS:

Theatre criticism should have a sense of discovery about the form. In Britain a lot of criticism is stuck in the mentality of judgement and very rarely expresses the joy of discovering art form. Most printed criticism would probably suggest to a visitor to London from another planet that theatre here was not a very live form. It's very hard for the critical establishment, which is used to assessing ideas of literary and aesthetic merit, to suddenly write about a new type of theatre experience and to take the risk of expressing surprise and discovery. So I don't think it's anyone's fault. In London everyone assumes that you are doing well as a theatre, if you get reviewed by Paul Taylor, Michael Billington, Benedict Nightingale, Michael Coveney, or John Peter. But BAC is a venue which promotes lots of experimental work and there's no real reason why I should try and get those people to see a kind of work that they might be completely unfamiliar with. We need to assess where the media outlets are that engage with the kind of work we are making.

ADRIAN NOBLE:

I often find criticism invaluable. But you have to be sceptical when they praise you. They'll say, "This is the best production of *Midsummer Night's Dream* in the last 20 years," and they'll say it next year about someone else . . . They should be able to set up an intellectual framework of the theatre and put every piece of theatre in a historical context. We, theatre practitioners, expect from the critics consistency of judgement and taste. We expect objectivity and an intellectual grasp of subject. We expect research and an intellectually constructive analysis of what we've done. Perhaps we expect too much . . . What's very annoying to theatre practitioners is the randomly arbitrary criticism and criticism which is individualistic, quirky, and gossipy . . . Critics have to be seekers in a way. That's part of their job. If there is an interesting writer, they should support him.

TREVOR NUNN:

Real criticism must be related to a context in which the critic declares his or her priorities. Then there should be a view of the art form and its history, and a view of its place or significance. Most of what we have at present is only a superficial response. In America it's much more stridently the case than it's here: the journalists writing about the Broadway scene are required to say, "Thumbs up!" or "Thumbs down!" At least here there are 10 or so national papers as well as the weekly and weekend newspapers, and a much wider variety of opinion gets published.

SUE ROLFE:

The main job of the critic is to try and find new audiences, and to appeal to the general man in the street. Criticism should also stimulate and excite the public to explore new forms of production. Unfortunately too often it is more the personal taste of the individual critics.

JOY SAPIEKA:

Ideally from a review you should get a sense that somebody has been through an experience, wants to re-live it through the pages, and is relating to you whether the experience is good or bad. What it is is varied: sometimes you get a sense of that, sometimes you get a sense of somebody showing off their knowledge, and sometimes you get a plot outline with a few comments in the end. I read so many reviews that I can almost tell in advance what I'm going to get.

ARNOLD WESKER:

A distinction should be made between criticism and reviewing. The reviewer, by and large, has to answer a different set of criteria than the critic who writes books of criticism. The function of the reviewer is to inform the public. There are many people who say, "Reading the reviews is the only way I can know about what's happening". The reviewers have to also excite the public. Someone like John Peter at *The Sunday Times*, for example, is excessively praising and excessively vindictive because he imagines that extreme views excite. But since newspaper reviewing is one person's opinion magnified out of proportion by print, I think there should be a warning at the top of every review, "This review could damage your perception of the play!"

Serious criticism should be an attempt to understand what the writer has done and somehow to communicate that to the public. You'll very rarely find a critic who is perceptive enough to see all that you've put into your work. This is what most writers look for: not necessarily praise, but someone who seems to understand what it is they're trying to do, and then comment. For example – I give my works to friends, relatives, people in the profession before I'm finished. They are the best critics. I don't always accept their criticism. But if something sounds right, then I make changes.

One of the few critics who attempts to understand is Michael Billington. He was astonishingly perceptive about my plays both in praise and in criticism. One would also like to find in criticism a sense of history of what has been achieved in the past, so that a perspective can be drawn. On the other hand, perspectives are often confused for comparisons and so the smart-arsed critic will say, "We don't have Shakespeare here". There seems to be a delight in hitting young writers over the head with the past. If this frame of reference is used as a battering ground to hit the writer over the head, then – yes, this is useless.

There is a strange phenomenon, which seems to apply to all the intermediators – publishers, directors, actors, gallery owners. It is that they often confuse themselves for those whom they represent . . .

Artists don't mind criticism.

PETER WILKINS:

I have seen plays and I have thought I could not understand what I've seen. Then I read Michael Billington or Irving Wardle the next day and they explain what I've seen. That's what criticism should be at its best. It should illuminate what the critic has seen and that should be conveyed to the reader so that it should make you say, "Oh, I really have got to see this play," or "I don't have to see it."

4

THE ROLE OF THEATRE CRITICISM IN THE THEATRE PROCESS: THE CRITICS' VIEW

Paul Allen
Kate Bassett
Michael Billington
James Christopher
Michael Coveney
Nick Curtis
Nicholas de Jongh
Jane Edwards
John Elsom
Lyn Gardner
Robert Gore-Langton
John Gross
Bill Hagerty

Ian Herbert
Robert Hewison
Jeremy Kingston
Alastair Macaulay
Sheridan Morley
David Nathan
Benedict Nightingale
John Peter
Ian Shuttleworth
Charles Spencer
Jack Tinker
Matt Wolf

They answer the question:

– If the theatre process consists of theatre makers, their works of art – theatre, the reality theatre reflects, and the audience, where does the critic come in this circle? Or in other words: what is and should be the role of the critic in the overall theatre process?

PAUL ALLEN:

I'm not sure where the critic's role begins or ends, but I'm absolutely certain that there is a place for the critics in that circle. Theatre is a collaboration between the audience and the performing company. For me the critic is the most heightened, the most intense and alert member of the audience. So if there is a collaboration going on, part of the role is to collaborate with more intellectual and emotional energy than everybody else. That's what I think should be done. It's unforgivable if a critic falls asleep or doesn't pay attention, and some critics don't pay attention very much. Some of them spend their time in the theatre working out what they're going to say rather than concentrating on the work first ... I do go to the theatre hoping it's going to be at least a distinctive experience. So I define reporting as urging people to go to the theatre, or saving them from going to non-distinctive and boring works. It's in that area we probably take our place. We also have a very simple straight-forward responsibility of mediating the relationship theatre has to society as a whole. Theatre transmits society's own experience back to it: it lives with it, analyzes it, maybe in the long term improves it and also copes with the emotional often very disturbing traumas that we go through.

Critics are there in the circle partly to explain why things work or not. It's also important for the critic to know that the readers don't like the critic saying, "I'm a superior human being" to the playwright, the director, and the actors. They don't like condescension on his part. At the BBC we try to respond to that, covering things which are serious without being patronizing.

KATE BASSETT:

I suppose, predominantly, you are a member of the audience. You are sitting there with everyone else watching the show. Maybe you have more expertise than occasional theatre-goers – more productions to compare to this one. Perhaps you are a bit more analytical than some spectators – because you are aware you have to write about the production immediately afterwards. But the image of the theatre critic just sitting there coldly assessing is wrong. You are entertained and emotionally moved along with everyone else.

The critic, afterwards, articulates what ideas the theatre piece is exploring and pinpoints how it achieves its effects (how it is moving or hilarious or disturbing, for example). Hopefully, a review gives some non-theatre-goers vicarious enrichment. However, where you come in the circle is mainly in encouraging members of the public to go and see a show – or in warning them it's bad. Longer term, critics describe an ephemeral event for posterity.

A review also gives creative talent public recognition. I think people in the theatre and film business take note of actors, directors and designers who get mentioned. Critics also keep theatre in the public eye. I hope this helps when theatre needs funding.

MICHAEL BILLINGTON:

Over the last three years most theatres have been drastically cut. So partly the critic's job now is to support proper funding for the theatre. There are other things I constantly champion as well. One cause I took up a long time ago was to broaden the band of plays that we saw in Britain. I don't say that my campaign necessarily has had a direct effect but I think there's much wider appreciation of world drama in British theatre than there used to be.

JAMES CHRISTOPHER:

Criticism comes in the very bottom. So actually it's a question of whom you're writing for. Sometimes the temptation is to write for the actor, the director, or the writer. But you should be writing for the audience. Ultimately you're paid to write for your readers. I believe there should be a dialogue with the theatre-makers. I'm not sure what the right form for that is. But you get some very interesting articles when theatre practitioners do put down their opinions.

MICHAEL COVENEY:

The critic is a part of the overall theatre process as an appointed member of the audience who has the privilege of articulating a response in print and being paid for it. The critic has to report the theatre and to measure it. To be a sounding board. There's all the different ways you can do that because there's all the levels of publications. I like the long case books too. John Lahr's casebook on *The Homecoming* by Harold Pinter, for instance. As a journalist I like using feature reviews, feature articles and profiles based on interviews, to extend the work of criticism, and complement it.

NICK CURTIS:

The most useful role of criticism is to point the audience towards that which is good and spur talent on a very basic level. One would very occasionally come across an absolute gem and be able to say to people, "Here's an absolute gem, notice it!" In terms of negativity, I don't think bad theatre should be allowed to live. When a show is bad, it's absolutely justifiable if a critic does have a power of disposing of it. That said, I've never been convinced by the arguments that critics are to blame for closing shows, particularly musicals. Critics have slammed musicals which are still running and praised ones which have died. The audiences aren't stupid. I got asked at a seminar whether I felt that criticism should be furthering the art. I was with a friend who used to be a critic and is now artistic director of BAC and both of us were saying, "No. It's the practitioners' job to further the art form and for us to recognize it."

NICHOLAS DE JONGH:

It's very sad to say so but theatre critics in England today have a negligible function. The commercial theatre is in a real decline, and again and again productions arrive in the West End, get very bad reviews from critics, and producers just provide more of this bad theatre. This rather suggests that critics don't have an impact on the commercial stage. On the other hand, look at the RSC and The National Theatre: The National Theatre under Richard Eyre has produced a tremendous series of famous twenty century plays, whereas the RSC, which is in steep decline, does a little European drama. This does suggest we are not very influential in changing what theatre practitioners wish to do too. It's my impression that theatre practitioners principally see critics as the means by which they get larger audiences and they hope to advance their reputations. They are not interested in and ignore negative criticism. There isn't a real interplay between practitioners and critics.

JANE EDWARDS:

Theatre critics are very powerful and they shouldn't abuse their power. Equally there is no point in over-praising productions to be kind and putting people off ever going to the theatre again. Actors get annoyed when they are endlessly compared to other actors who appeared in the same roles in the past but that's an important part of the process as long as one doesn't get too nostalgic about the past. It's important that critics should make a fuss if they feel that standards are slipping, in verse speaking for instance.

Although *Time Out* covers the entire area of the fringe theatre I don't want us to be hand-in-glove with the fringe. At the same time I don't want us to miss out on new young talent. In that sense I do feel I have a mission as a critic. Otherwise, one's job would simply be a question of acting as a guide: "My aunt's coming up from the country, what should I take her to see?" There's nothing very mission-like about that.

JOHN ELSOM:

On one level, the theatre critics are an important filter for the impressions they get from the theatre and they have to create and retain a kind of credibility with their public. I remember Harold Hobson was a reliable filter. I've a great admiration for Irving Wardle now and some others. On another level, criticism is trying to develop the public debate by which values are formed. You may find, as Tynan said, that the good critic is the one who says what hasn't been done. Therefore it's difficult to be loved if you are a critic. You'll lose your friends in the theatre. You've got to be strong-minded enough to be able to take the periods when what you're saying is extremely unpopular.

LYN GARDNER:

Theatre criticism has many roles. Partly it is a consumer-guide. But to a large extent it also gives people the feeling of the event. By its very nature criticism serves the purpose of noting that the event happened. There are huge responsibilities to the theatre makers as well. After all the truth is that we come in, watch a play, and spend a couple of hours writing about something that represents a year or two years of somebody's work. I honestly do believe that the critic should take that very seriously. Of course, it depends on your background. If, like me, you've spent a lot of your early career seeing companies at very early stages of their work, you know that there is a symbiotic relationship between critics and the practitioners. Magazines like *City Limits* had a very nurturing role because the only review a show would get would be there. That's helpful because it offers people the attention to get funding. At a later stage the national critics would say, "Oh, this is wonderful work!" but actually it has been going on for, say, five years. So perhaps my experience at the *City Limits* is the reason I feel there is more responsibility. I don't feel the same responsibility if I go along and see Adrian Noble's *Midsummer Nights' Dream* at the RSC or a Richard Eyre show at the National – it jolly well should be good, and obviously if it isn't – you say so.

But criticism in a company's early stages can be an absolutely vital sounding board because it's almost the only outside and independent eye that they have because their audiences are usually friends, or friends of friends. You write differently about a first play that is going on at the fringe theatre and a first play that is at the Royal Court or the Bush Theatre. Of course, critics take these things into account.

ROBERT GORE-LANGTON:

The role of the critic is to bring alive the pleasure of theatre-going. The critic is a mediator between the theatre and would-be audience. You write as much for the people who don't go to the theatre as you do for the people who do go. I've heard it said that the critic should write for other critics. I'm not happy about that. If you regard theatre as a specialist activity for a small audience, then you run into trouble. I see myself as a part of the newspaper business rather than a part of the theatre business. But a good critic will make a point of getting to see things that are off the beaten track because if we have a duty to the theatre, it's really doing the legwork: getting out to see what's on offer. And quite a few critics don't.

JOHN GROSS:

One of my favorite stories about literary criticism, but it applies equally to theatre, is a story about Joseph Conrad. His wife wrote a little memoir of him and she described one morning, late in his career, when the first review of his new novel had appeared in *The Times*. It wasn't very good. She brought the paper to him and said, "There's a review of your novel in the newspaper, dear." "Well?" – he asked. She said, "Well, it's got some criticism but it's very constructive criticism." And suddenly the mask cracked and the great man, who had endured so much in his life, burst out, "I don't want constructive criticism, I want praise!" If Joseph Conrad could say that ... In some ways performers and artist, of every kind have an almost physiological need of praise. Therefore there is a potential hostility between them and the critic – any critic. Some actors say they never read reviews. I find it hard to believe. I should add that I also write books, so I know what it is to be reviewed – to be on the receiving end.

BILL HAGERTY:

It depends very much on for whom you're writing, doesn't it? The sort of paper I work for is for people who want to know basically whether it's worth going to see or not. As for the theatre-makers: I'm not going to pretend for a minute that in the theatre process it would matter if nobody ever read a thing I wrote again. They read me and hopefully find they are entertained, but they are not going to find anything profound in my work that will aid the theatre process at all. However, that's not true of Michael Coveney, or Benedict Nightingale, or Charles Spencer, who can make people laugh but are fulfilling a different and important function at the same time. Certainly those people have got to be part of the theatre process. That's why they are invited on the lecture platforms to interview directors or actors.

IAN HERBERT:

If you place the critic between the theatre-maker and the audience, saying that they are there to interpret, that's much too vain. The good theatre production needs no critic to tell you what a wonderful experience it is – you go there and you have it. But because theatre is a one-off, live event, there are always a lot of people who haven't been there and want to know what it was like. The critics have that recording role, and of course they have an interpretative role too. I see the critic as a member of the audience who has seen more theatre than the others, and is able to help future audiences to grasp some of the feeling, even the meaning as he sees it, of the experience he's been through.

ROBERT HEWISON:

The theatre critic represents the tribune of the people. He or she does not represent the profession. Obviously by seeing many plays we have quite a reasonable knowledge about how theatre works but our function is not to interfere.

JEREMY KINGSTON:

Criticism has a vital role: it helps the audience, it clears the decks of rubbish for better work coming in. Also: we're reaching a time when perhaps more people go to the major theatres. I like to feel that we're offering them the opportunity to see plays in fringe theatres too. And of course, with *The Times* people like to read about a play, even if they're not going to come up from Cornwall to London to see it.

Regarding the theatre-makers: I think generally some actors and directors do not read theatre criticism because it puts them off. But our criticisms could well affect a production. When I met for the first time Katie Mitchell, she had just produced *Endgame* at the Donmar. She asked me what I thought about it. "I have the feeling," I said, "it's ten minutes too long". She asked at what point I had felt that. When I named a particular speech by Hamm, she was very interested because they had found that this was a place where people started getting restless ... Once I saw a Chinese play *Porcelain* in an obscure North London fringe theatre. I didn't even want to go to it but the company's press representative urged me to. I was very impressed, and wrote a very positive review. Then the play transferred to the Theatre Upstairs. When that happens I feel I've actually helped a production rise, or helped a career. Another example of the critics' role in the theatre is the musical *Martin Guerre*: the critics' opinion caused a lot of rewrites in it in order to get it into a better shape. So critics can help theatre-makers especially of the subsidized companies or one of the rich companies. A fringe play doesn't have time.

ALASTAIR MACAULAY:

We are a part of the audience. That's all. The audience is going to talk about the show anyway. We are simply there to help stimulate and inform the discussion. And we may be no more correct than other members of the audience – though we should try to be. I'm not interested in the aspect of theatre criticism that is there to sell tickets. I'm not interested in trying to force more people into the theatre. I just want them to have more inquiring minds about theatre, whether or not they go to the theatre. Nor do I write for performers or playwrights or directors: they read reviews at their own peril. For the general reader, the critic acts as a prism – maybe distorting but, ideally, intensifying aspects of the work of art, making it a keener experience.

Once I was introduced to an actress at a party. After a minute, she asked for my name again and I told her it.

"Alastair Macaulay!" she yelled, and she started to hit me, not entirely in jest. "You gave me the worst review I ever had!" The room was full of other critics and theatre folk, and everyone was looking. And she carried on: "And what makes it **worse**," (she was still hitting me)" is that you were absolutely **right**!"

I've had other theatre folk tell me I was right, sometimes in less embarrassing circumstances, but so what? Being right doesn't make you a good critic, though it helps. I like critics who are illuminating, even when I disagree with them.

You go on discovering new aspects of yourself as you write. I also teach dance history, and, when I was 31, a new student of mine said, "You're not at all like what I expected you to be from reading you." Unwisely, I asked her what she had thought I would be like. "Old and fat," she said. "And very happy."

SHERIDAN MORLEY:

We live in a very small country and in the theatre-going community everybody knows everybody. We use the same restaurants, we tend to meet at the same parties, so it's very rare that you'll find a critic who doesn't know a great many actors and playwrights. It's a volatile community and we don't have that separation of powers that they have in the States. For example, since I come from a family of actors, I have actors, directors and playwrights who are friends, and they come to my house but they know that I reserve the right to attack them in print. It works very well, people get used to the fact that we review them – favourably or unfavourably. More and more actors and directors are now taking to print and they write very well, and if you write a hostile review, they are capable of writing back to the papers. So you get a rather good debate going on, not only between critics but between actors and critics.

DAVID NATHAN:

The critic comes in as a guide to his audience – the readers. He should tell them when something is worthwhile spending money on. The critic has no duty to posterity. But it's nice that there is a general body of informed observers who are looking out for what is best all the time. If they praise what is best and dispraise what is worst, then surely the general effect over the years is for the cheap to be winnowed out and for the best to be encouraged. So in the end it affects theatre itself.

BENEDICT NIGHTINGALE:

It's a very tricky subject. Your prime obligation as a theatre critic is not to help theatre, except insofar as that it's very good for your readers. To that extent, yes, of course, you want to help to improve the theatre. But it's rather dangerous if you think of yourself too strongly as someone who's there for the good of the theatre. If you're not careful you may begin to neglect the other more primary role of criticism – the discourse with your readership. The two are not in contradiction however. I'd like to feel that my general attitudes do become part of the theatre process. I don't delude myself though that it happens very much or very strongly. What you do is: you add to a feeling about culture – its health or non-health. That was the case with Tynan when he was saying that the British theatre took no interest in the world around it. He made people feel dissatisfied with the drama at the time. But he didn't cause *Look Back in Anger*. He helped to cause the conditions in which it could flourish.

JOHN PETER:

You can't help remembering that the following morning the actor who is playing Macbeth is going to read what you've written about his work. He ought to feel that you understand his work and your criticism is based on knowledge. But I don't think it's my job to cheer up people in the acting profession. My job is to tell the reader as objectively as I can what my personal opinion was. My relationship to the acting profession should take a low priority. There's one other thing: to what extent you conform to the social and political assumptions of the newspaper that you write for. It has once been said about me that I express certain opinions because I know that this is what Rupert Murdoch's readers would like. I was hurt by that remark because it came from someone I respect. But I can see that this could be a problem: if you think that your editors expect a certain approach, you can start censoring yourself. It can happen without you noticing it. Anyone who knows anything about Eastern Europe will know that people can change their minds and not realize they'd done so. This is probably the most destructive type of corruption. This is a problem that few people in Western Europe understand because they've seldom had to function under such restraints or threats. But in fact most newspapers don't mind what you say politically: the British have consistently underestimated the impact of the arts on politics.

IAN SHUTTLEWORTH:

The short answer is: the critic's duty is to all of these things. So it becomes a question of how you apportion those factors. A critic's first duty is to the readers of the paper the critic works on. He or she has to convey both an impression of the event as it is and some kind of an opinion about it to the readers, and the style of writing should also be relevant to that particular constituency. Then we get into the duties to the theatre practitioners and to what you call reality. The duty to the practitioners is the most problematic of all because we move in the same circles and have the same sensibilities and theatrical experiences. But the fact remains that we are journalists rather than theatre practitioners.

CHARLES SPENCER:

I don't think there's any social use of theatre criticism at all. If a show gets good reviews, it's likely to sell more tickets. If it gets bad reviews, it's likely to close quickly. I wouldn't like to claim much more than that. Basically you're trying to guide your readers to a decent evening out and a satisfying show. I don't see myself as laying down the law on what people ought to see. The important thing about the job is to be as open-minded as possible and have a broad variety of tastes. One of the few things I feel slightly evangelical about is that popular entertainment doesn't get nearly as fair a crack of the whip as it ought to. This is wrong. There is a great danger that critics will start living in ivory towers. They know everything that is happening at the RSC but they don't have a clue what's happening on TV.

JACK TINKER:

Criticism is a very honorable part of the whole. Without the critics you wouldn't have the audience or you certainly wouldn't have the audience in sufficient numbers. Criticism generates or should generate an excitement and anticipation for the theatre. That's what it did for me in the North of England. I couldn't afford to come down to London as a 12-year old boy but I felt that I was a part of what was going on because I had been let into it by the critics. They did allow me to put my nose up against the window and be a part of the whole debate. I'm writing for those people who haven't yet seen the show but who might be stimulated and interested in what's going on. I'm writing it for myself as I was this 12-year old boy. People who live in London are very privileged – they just come down to the West End. But most people don't live here and I feel that I'm opening the window for them.

MATT WOLF:

I hope the critic is playing a kind of benevolently skeptical role in the theatre process. Benevolently, because you would be foolish to deny the process exists but sceptical because somehow you cannot be caught up in it. There's more pressure now on critics to be a part of the process whether they want to be or not. But you need to maintain a bit of distance and remember that you are not of the industry, you are not on the payroll of Cameron Mackintosh or the Shubert organization or the National Theatre. You are answerable to your own publication and to yourself. I'm absolutely not one of those people who think you need experience of the profession in order to be a critic. On the other hand, I don't fanatically believe that you can't socialize with people in the profession.

5

THE ROLE OF THEATRE CRITICISM IN THE THEATRE PROCESS: THE THEATRE-MAKERS' VIEW

Playwrights:

Sir Alan Ayckbourn
Steven Berkoff
David Edgar

Directors:

Howard Davies
Sir Richard Eyre
David Farr
Sir Peter Hall
Jonathan Kent
Katie Mitchell
Saw Mendes
Adrian Noble
Trevor Nunn
Max Stafford-Clark

Producers:

Thelma Holt
Sir Cameron Mackintosh
Michael Morris
Tom Morris
Peter Wilkins

Press-Agents and a Publisher:

Sharon Kean
Sue Hyman
Nick Hern
Sue Rolfe
Joy Sapieka

They answer the question:

– If the theatre process consists of theatre makers, their works of art – theatre, the reality theatre reflects, and the audience, where does the critic come in this circle? Or in other words: what is and should be the role of the critic in the overall theatre process?

SIR ALAN AYCKBOURN:

Obviously, the critic is a link between the audience and the artists. When you are in a big urban centre such as London, there are thousands of things going on all the time, events, shows, exhibitions. That's where the critic comes in. To bring them to your attention. To direct you through doorways you might otherwise have missed. That's how I view them as a member of the public. As a practitioner, though, critics rarely if ever affect my work quite so directly. Actually, by the time they get round to criticizing a play of mine, I'm probably writing another one. I usually know what's wrong with the play they are currently reviewing as well as they do. So it doesn't make a vast deal of difference to me what they think. Not in the short term. In the long term, ah, well maybe. But the people who really tell me about my play in the end, of course, are the audiences.

STEVEN BERKOFF:

Critics are there to spread the word. They are there to keep the good word. They're there to see, to have a vision, to recognize, to find out before the public, to discern. Many critics go year after year to the theatre, they sit there for hours seeing simple fare and the danger of that is that after many years they become institutionalized. They start thinking everything is all right. Then they come to see me and they vomit because they are used to prison food. The senses of a good critic are to amplify the experience, to give it air, to give it enthusiasm. Because we can't live without theatre. Theatre does create an environment where people can sit together. Theatre and music draw groups, they gather many hundreds of people. The only other gathering of many hundreds of people are sport events or the numbing pop concert. You can read a book by yourself but this doesn't unite you to other people. The critic must be the messenger, he must give out. He must attack when it really is detrimental, but without cruelty.

HOWARD DAVIES:

The role of the critic should be to educate the public: if, for example, you only come to London once a year to see theatre, you read newspapers and magazines in order to stay in touch with the events politically and culturally. Therefore the critic is an important guide and point of entry for a lot of people who don't see theatre. He's not just somebody writing a listing saying what to go and see. The critic should be able to inform people about the play, place it in a cultural context, and be able to draw parallels and make social and political connections. That requires some courage. If I was opening my newspaper in the Lake District, and I didn't come to London for the most of the year, I'd be bored by what I read because I'd feel excluded. The critics are addressing a very small group of London theatre-goers and are basically writing towards the profession. I don't think they are really addressing their readership.

DAVID EDGAR:

Critics can observe and describe from a particular position of knowledge the relationship between a constantly changing reality and the tradition, and the expectations that arise out of that tradition. They have a role of mediating. They could facilitate an understanding of why it was, for instance, that in the '80s and the '90s a lot of people wanted to write plays about gambling and killing.

SIR RICHARD EYRE:

If you see the theatre process as a circle, you'd have to say that a segment of the circumference includes theatre criticism. Without the mediation of the critic between the practitioner the audience the circle wouldn't be complete. There is a need for the mediators to exist.

DAVID FARR:

I've never experienced theatre criticism as a part of the process. What theatre criticism can do is to give to the creative individual an overall sense of a form and a journey of where a movement might be going. In the realm of the new writing, for example, one does occasionally see evidence of criticism trying to draw together the individual voices into a movement attempting to say something about the way we live. But sometimes in its search of a unity, it threatens to encourage a kind of homogeneity where a voice that doesn't fit into the stream of critical and theatrical thought of the moment is rejected. Whereas some of those voices are in fact the most exciting ones. That is then recovered by the critical consciousness. One can take examples of Strindberg or Ibsen, who were defied first and later accepted. No one ever learns that lesson. Perhaps that's the lesson the critics have to learn.

SIR PETER HALL:

Of course, critics help the theatre because at the least they tell people it's on. They tell people what's happening. They create a climate of opinion . . . I did the first English production of *Waiting for Godot*. It got the most dreadful reviews with the exception of one by Harold Hobson. Not only did he recognize Beckett at the first viewing, he recognized Pinter and Arden and Osborne. I don't think he missed anybody. One of the most famous productions I did in the '60s was *Hamlet* at the RSC in Stratford, with David Warner. It ran for two years and was the *Hamlet* of the decade, but it received only one good notice from Ronald Bryden of *The New Statesman*. Does this mean that critics are wrong? No, it means the critics were wrong in these two instances . . . All of us are paranoid in the theatre and tend to believe that critics talk with each other and decide together not to like or to like something. That simply isn't true . . . Of course, I read the notices. Most people do even when they say they don't. But you have to read reviews at an arm's length. Particularly if they are good, because then you start thinking you're good. That's very dangerous indeed. I don't believe anything is worthwhile in the arts unless it's absolutely terrifying as you start each piece of work. I bet any artist will tell you the same thing. Probably the greater the artist, the more the terror.

NICK HERN:

Critics have got a very small role to play. They are a convenience for people who go to the theatre. Theatre criticism is pretty transient and ephemeral. But since it's the only record of what it was actually like to be at a particular show at a particular time, it has more value. That's what dignifies it.

THELMA HOLT:

The critic is part of our process. He is not the enemy, nor is he inaccessible. Of course, I find it disappointing if I have a bad review, but that is a professional hazard. The critic often brings a fresh eye to a production, which can inform the actors and the director. Constructive criticism is productive, but I disapprove of destructive criticism very strongly.

When a critic has not done his homework in those circumstances where homework is required, (e.g. where he is seeing a piece of work, for instance, that has come from a part of the work where people have been disadvantaged in regard to what is happening on the world stage) a good critic takes this into consideration. Some years ago we brought Ian Caramitru's *Hamlet* to the Royal National Theatre. There were things about that production which could have been considered a little passé. The director and the actors had been influenced in their attitude towards the play by the horrendous cirucmstances under which they were then living in Romania. Not all critics took this into consideration, and we received some reviews which I thought lacked sensitivity to a world situation.

SUE HYMAN:

I don't think the critic is representative of the audience at all. I do think the playwright and the company need criticism because they need to know where their work is. Interestingly enough however good an actor is and known on TV, what comes for them when you talk with an agent is their theatre reviews. It's a prestige as well. Certainly Trevor Nunn and Andrew Lloyd Webber remember all their reviews . . . Critics do have enormous influence on the initial stages of a production's life. The reviews have a huge effect on all the ticket agents.

SHARON KEAN:

Theatre criticism's role is partly to publicize theatre because theatre is a very expensive past-time and there has to be something that helps people choose what to spend 50 pounds on. People who produce theatre see the critic as almost the enemy, or certainly somebody they have to convince and persuade. But we – agents – don't see them like that. I believe that every single night a critic goes to the theatre hoping it will be good.

JONATHAN KENT:

Speaking as somebody who runs a theatre, I see it as a way of disseminating the news of the play. Especially as we don't have huge marketing budget, it's a form of editorial publicity. But in a purer sense, it should be a record of a crucial artistic strand of the nation. We are still a theatrical nation and theatre is still the repository of our national soul. So critics have a responsibility which I really don't think they always fulfill. Nowadays, more and more, criticism is "This is terrible! Don't see it!" Or, "This is brilliant! See it!" It's a pity if theatre criticism is simply this. Theatre criticism is going through some sort of a crisis now. But just as a nation is supposed to get the government it deserves, perhaps a theatre gets the criticism it deserves.

SIR CAMERON MACKINTOSH:

I do think criticism has a place in the circle. If we didn't have any theatre critics at all, newspapers would not find a reason to publicize most shows. They are an essential part of how a show becomes known. Sometimes you get really brilliant critics who have such a gift for writing themselves that they can convey their enthusiasm, and that compels somebody to buy a ticket. Frank Rich was one of the most brilliant modern theatre critics. He wrote as well as the best playwrights he was reviewing but when he got disillusioned with writing for the theatre, his criticisms were not as interesting because he simply wasn't excited anymore.

SAM MENDES:

Criticism is a part of what theatre is. It always has been. I've never seen Kean or Olivier act but I've read about them. I've never seen the original version of *The Birthday Party* but I've read Harold Hobson. I've learned about my theatre heritage through the critics. In retrospect it brings me great pleasure to read about other people's shows. Criticism is a mutually beneficial relationship. Our work is meaningless unless it's interpreted on a broad canvass. In theory it should be a very fulfilling two-way process: we get publicity from the critics and they watch our work over a number of years. They can judge it in context. In recent years, as theatre has come increasingly under pressure financially, it's been more and more necessary for practitioners to get good reviews. So criticism has become a little less aggressive. That's good on the one hand, because one's ego is left bruised at times when criticism is negative. However, on the other hand, it can backfire if the public begins to mistrust endlessly good reviews. I basically feel supported by the press. Of course, there have been occasions when I wanted desperately to go to a critic and propagate an act of physical violence on him. But that's criticism's function: it's an act of live debate and the basis for debate is disagreement.

KATIE MITCHELL:

Theatre happens in the audience and a critic is a part of that audience. So their moral responsibility is to act as a bridge or filter through which they transmit their experience for those who haven't been there. However I'm not always certain that critics do that.

MICHAEL MORRIS:

Critics are an important part of the theatre process – facilitating, enlightening, helping the public to understand theatre. Like producers, they have to be a bridge between a work of art and its audience. I wouldn't go as far as saying theatre doesn't exist without critics. It exists because what makes a show succeed is not what critics say but what the audience says. Word of mouth is the oldest and best form of publicity in the world. But critics are a part of that process. In the business you see them a lot and you either decide you're not going to have a relationship with them because that would compromise your work and their work, or you decide the reverse. From the very start of my work I decided that I wanted to build bridges with some of these people as I feel they are part of the community. I am always happy to tell them informally about my planning.

ADRIAN NOBLE:

At best there is a very creative and responsible relationship between the artist and the critic, the general public and the critic. Fortunately, because of the nature of the press in this country, we – in the arts – have much more independence from criticism than artists have in America. A critic here can't close a show and therefore we are not in their claws in that way. It doesn't mean that they don't try to do it. Some theatre critics do. But the best are read by actors and directors with respect. They take in all their comments and sometimes adjust accordingly. But we have to accept that they are secondary to the process. The process happens between the artist and the audience.

TREVOR NUNN:

It would be nice if criticism were a part of the circle and not tangential to the circle, or a satellite completely outside of the circle. I've read Russian theatre criticism which is very lengthy, considerate, and sort of divided into three sections – a full investigation of the text, an investigation of the new concept, and the third section is about individual performance and achievement. Nothing in that detail or with that thoroughness exists in writing about the theatre here. In England it's often the case that most of the critics don't like something, but they don't like it each for very different reasons. That's a good thing in terms of having a broad spectrum but it's not something on which one could base a re-assessment of the production. I've gone back into rehearsal because of something I've read in a critical piece. But I don't think many people doing new plays or revivals would consult that sort of journalism to gain clues about how the work might be improved, or to gain fresh insights, because journalism invariably doesn't operate on the same level on which the production has been undertaken.

Critics should be like gardeners: many different plants and flowers poke their way through the soil of the garden, and it's possible that many of them can live if they are in some way encouraged and nurtured. That's something that I wrote to Frank Rich some years ago when he was the critic for *The New York Times*. Actually that's the biggest contention that I've ever been in with a critic. At the time he also took over the columns of *The New York Sunday Times*, so there was no other voice in *The New York Times*. And since that was the only newspaper that was read by people who were likely to go to the theatre, that was a case of monopoly. I would have thought under those circumstances that a critic would need to find some generosity of spirit but it was really quite the contrary. Frank Rich was a man who at the time seemed to be intoxicated with the idea that he did have this power of life and death over shows, and he decreed that most things should not live. I wrote to him about how his garden grew and that it was a very dead garden. It had hardy perennials – musicals that had been around for years, which he hadn't tended. But he had extinguished most of the other flowers. So it was a patch in which almost nothing grew. Obviously he was very angered. He was hysterical. We spoke on the telephone a couple of times and he pointed out that in his view he had to be subject to his own integrity, and secondly he thought many things were growing and would bear increasing fruit in future years. But I don't think that was the case. I don't think there's many things that did come to flourish. What happened instead was that producing managements got more timid, they tried to second guess what he would feel, and more and more of them grew tired. The imagination and daring to initiate something for Broadway was almost extinguished at that time.

SUE ROLFE:

Theatre criticism is part of the publicity machine.

JOY SAPIEKA:

Critics' role is to give people an idea of a particular production. Criticism should be a guide as to whether they should go through this experience and whether they would enjoy it. Although, of course, a review is by definition subjective as it is only one person's point of view. In my experience, word of mouth is the strongest way of selling anything, followed by publicity and promotion. Criticism, depending on whether it is positive or negative, can either boost these or counter them.

MAX STAFFORD-CLARK:

Criticism is a necessary and inevitable part of theatre. It would be impossible to do without it. The opinions that respond to your play are the peer group opinion, the critics' opinion, the public opinion and posterity. It's the peer group opinion that's most important to me. But in the end criticism is the front line of response. . . . Commercially criticism is essential because without consensus of good reviews you don't get the house full.

TOM MORRIS:

Everyone knows that live bits of culture work by word of mouth: you hear about some experience, you trust the person who's telling you about it, and you go to that place. Critics are part of that process. They just have very loud voices. They are essentially gossip writers who reflect whatever aspects of the theatrical experience they want to. Live theatre is an imaginative collaboration between the theatre makers and the audience: the theatre-makers invite the audience to imagine something together. The critics are a part of the audience.

PETER WILKINS:

In the commercial theatre the critics' role is literally to advertise the fact that the play is on and to give some idea of what that experience has been. You don't look to a critic to tell you whether you did it properly or not. You look at criticism to see if you are accessible, not if you're artistically succeeding or not.

Part IV
Move Over, Tarantino!
(14 "True Crime" Stories From
The Critics' Lives)

COUP DE TOILETTE

Kate Bassett

I should probably confess to having smashed a perfectly nice toilet to smithereens on the opening night of a West End show. This wasn't, I hasten to add, a critical reaction to the show – though it certainly looked like a hatchet job. There I was just innocently pulling the chain and next thing I knew the cistern was off the wall, careering past my nose and landing in the bowl below with a crash and a whopping splash. I'd had a near squeak. Who knows, maybe it was all a cunning set-up by the management ... "London critic meets dramatic end in interval. Coup de toilette".

DON'T TOUCH THE UNTOUCHABLES!

Kate Bassett

My most nightmarish moment in a theatre was probably reviewing an awful soft porn male strip show – a kind of sub-Chippendales affair – that was touring Britain. I was, as critics usually are, seated at the end of a row. Little did I know this was going to involve audience participation. One of the performers, flaunting only a G-string and an array of quite unnecessary muscles, was suddenly sprinting up the aisle and standing astride my chair, gyrating his various bulges in my face and starting to pull me up towards the stage. My critical biro and spiral-bound notepad had never served me better. One flash of those and he retired pretty sharpish – thank Christ.

SELECTED FOR REVENGE

Michael Billington

20 years ago, at the Royal Court, there was a play by David Storey – *Mother's Day*, which I disliked. David Storey is a very fine dramatist and novelist but I said the play's a stinker. I wasn't alone – most critics thought it was below Storey's best form. About two nights later, I was going through the Royal Court bar on my way to the other theatre and David Storey was there waiting for all the critics. He is a massive and heavily built man, 16 stones. He accosted us as we passed by and he seized me and started, as I thought, to playfully tap the back of my head. Then I realized he was giving me a sort of cuffing. He was attacking me physically on account of my opinions. And I stood there meekly, tamely accepting this. He didn't do it to anyone else. That's what angered me and puzzled me. Why didn't he attack Irving Wardle? Or Michael Coveney? Whoever? That incident was reported in the newspapers. Then I was constantly invited to go and talk on radio and TV programmes about what it's like to be beaten by David Storey. It grew out of proportion. It's silly but it always is in my mind when people talk about the relation of critics and artists.

A DEADLY COINCIDENCE

Michael Billington

Years ago I wrote a devastating review of the actress Mary Ure. It was an unusually rude review for me. The next morning I was walking to the West End and I saw billboards with *The Evening Standard* newspapers saying, "Mary Ure Dies." The first thought was, "Did she see that review and did she take her life?" A few people made that assumption. I subsequently discovered that she died of an overdose of pills and drink during the night, so she could never have seen the review. But it did make me more cautious after that about ever being abusive about any individual performer.

ON SUSPICION OF TERRORISM

James Christopher

In the film *White Heat* James Cagney stands on top of a giant gas tank and cries, "I'm on top of the world, mama!" I've always wanted to do that. So one night I did. I got drunk at a party and climbed the one next to the Oval cricket ground. Someone called the police. They thought I was carrying a bomb. I've got an Irish passport, so they thought I must be IRA. They arrested me on suspicion of terrorism. Two days later they let me out after interviews, search warrants, the lot.

A week later, at the Heathrow airport, I was on my way to Beijing to see a Chinese opera for the LIFT. When I was passing passport control, they took my number. The guard thought he'd hit the jackpot: an IRA suspect on his way to China to see a piece of theatre just a week after being arrested on suspicion of terrorism. They simply did not believe it at all and shut down airport for four hours and grilled me until about 4.00 am. Meanwhile a very angry plane load of passengers were waiting on the runway. In the end they had to let me go.

Being a theatre critic can have its unusual moments.

AN EYE FOR AN EYE

Nick Curtis

I have only been attacked once by an actor whom I hadn't actually reviewed but who accused me of giving him old-fashioned looks. This happened at the Lyric Studio. He wasn't doing his job properly which was probably why I had been giving him a slightly disapproving glance.

MISFORTUNE STRIKES TWICE

Robert Gore-Langton

Once in Edinburgh I went to see a new French play in the King's Theatre. Quarter of the way through the performance I had to go to the loo. I was desperate. I tried to get past all these people's knees but towards the end of the line I tripped on a woman's handbag, I fell over and cut my eye open on the ashtray. I was taken off to a nurse, who patched my eye up, and then I went back to the theatre at the interval. In the second half my back went into spasm and I couldn't move out of my seat except side ways. I was the last one in the theatre and I had to be lifted out by two ushers.

KGB IS COMING

Thelma Holt

Michael Coveney and I were coming back from what was then the Soviet Union. We were on the plane and the engines were turning. They suddenly stopped, and through the window we saw a black Mercedes approaching at a considerable speed. In those days such an event was a cause for general concern, and we were very nervous. I said to Coveney, "They have found out about your book". "No, they haven't", said Coveney. "They have found out about your diamond". At this point the doors of the aeroplane opened and in walked two Georgians with a case of wine for each of us. What a relief – I think I lost a couple of pounds in sheer fright.

DEATH THREATS AND REVERSAL OF FORTUNE

Nicholas de Jongh

I was threatened with murder by Steven Berkoff, but that's so well known it is too boring. He seemed very serious at the time, though he subsequently said that he wasn't. I'm very well disposed towards him now. And he to me. Or so it seems. You can never really know.

Playwrights, actors and directors regard us with the kind of respectful wariness that prison officers display when dealing with violent or disturbed criminals. Or does that sound too melodramatic? There's a grain of truth there, though.

THE BODY IS IN THE DIVAN

David Nathan

It was a very hot summer evening. I can't remember the name of the play but there were two great dames of the British theatre on the stage chatting to each other. The atmosphere was getting heavier and heavier, and I could see heads drooping all around me. A friend of mine, another critic, came in a quarter of an hour late, sat in the seat in front of me, and asked me what was happening. I said, "See that divan the two old ladies are sitting on. The body is in there". At the interval he, another critic and I went to a pub. We don't often talk about the play we are seeing but the critic, who was sitting in front of me said, "That was interesting the way they never mentioned the body in the divan they were sitting on." The other critic, whose eyes had been drooping, thought he had missed it ... I couldn't stop laughing, so I gave the game away.

A CRITIC STRIKES BACK

John Peter

When I was a free-lance critic I was invited to a performance by the Pip Simmons Group, a well-known fringe company. The show was about the Vietnam war and was written and created by the actors. I was not there to review it. In the first act, something which, wasn't actually a tear gas, but smelt and looked like it, was released. It rather upset me because I had been on the receiving end of a tear gas attack in Budapest in 1956. I still think it's infantile to do this to a theatre audience. This was in the Young Vic and I was sitting in a gangway seat. In the second half, at one point, actors came down the gangways with toy revolvers in their hands. The actor who came down my gangway put a pistol against my head. I asked him repeatedly to remove it. He said "Why, what's the matter? What's your problem?" I said, "My problem is that I don't like this". He insisted, so I finally got up and threw him down the gangway.

I don't think this is a funny story but it gives you a good picture of what used to be the naive side of British political theatre. It's done by grown-up adolescents who probably never suffered serious hardship and almost certainly never were at the receiving end of political violence.

A WOMANIZER UNDER SURVEILLANCE

Sue Rolfe

I had a friend who had come over from Hong Kong. She was going to be a journalist and there was a production of the RSC that she wanted to see that night. I had only one spare ticket – the other half of a critic's ticket. He was a well-known womanizer, so there she was and his hand kept creeping across her knee. Of course, he was making advances not knowing I had anything to do with her.

SIX INCHES APART FROM DEATH

Charles Spencer

When I was at Oxford, I was an assistant stage manager of a semi-professional opera production and I largely spent my time doing the donkey work. One day the woman who was meant to be running the show on the prompt corner was off and I had to do it. I couldn't read music, so I got completely lost. I had to press buttons for lighting and for flying down the scenery, and I got completely tangled about this. Instead of giving up I pressed a button and in the middle of the leading singer's big aria a set came zooming down from the flies and nearly killed him. It actually missed him by six inches. He stopped singing for a moment. There was a terrible silence and then the show went on. No one ever spoke to me again after that in that company. I had to help strike the set and at about 3 o'clock in the morning, when they had all gone off to their cast party, I was putting up the set for the next one. That's when I decided it was safer sitting on the other side.

NIGHTMARES IN DAYTIME

Matt Wolf

Once I got a call at the office. The voice said, "This is Stephen Berkoff". I thought it was a joke and that a specific friend was having me on, and I said "Oh, come off it." The voice seemed perplexed, "What do you mean – come off it?" I said, "It's not Steven Berkoff. It's this friend." "No, no. This is Steven Berkoff." The voice went on, "If you don't believe me, here's my number – you can call me back." Then he said, "I'm very interested in the fact that you seem not to like my work." And I don't actually like his work, having given his slow-motion National Theatre's *Salome* one of the few bad reviews that it got. "I'd like to take you to lunch to talk about it," he said. I had images of us meeting in a back alley somewhere in the East End where he would beat me up with ten of his friends, so I said, "Well, Mr. Berkoff, I don't really believe in meeting people I review good or bad. And I stand by what I wrote." "Well, if you change your mind, here's my number, call me," he said and hung up. But I didn't change my mind.

Part V
Diagnosis Of A Theatre

1

BRITISH THEATRE TODAY: THE CRITICS' REPORT

Paul Allen
Kate Bassett
Michael Billington
James Christopher
Michael Coveney
Nick Curtis
Nicholas de Jongh
Jane Edwards
John Elsom
Robert Gore-Langton
Peter Hepple
Ian Herbert

Robert Hewison
Jeremy Kingston
Alastair Macaulay
Sheridan Morley
David Nathan
Benedict Nightingale
John Peter
Ian Shuttleworth
Charles Spencer
Jack Tinker
Irving Wardle
Matt Wolf

They answer the questions:

– *What are the main strengths and weaknesses of the contemporary British theatre? What are the problems it faces today?*

PAUL ALLEN:

One of the enormous strengths of British theatre is the way in which it works with writers. We have a sort of saying in companies like the RSC, "You do every classical play as if it is a new play, and every new play as if it is a classic."

The problems are that our theatre structure was invented in the '60s and is now out-of-date. We have a whole series of theatre buildings around the country which soak in subsidy and leave only small sums for the development of the work. We pay for the stages and not for the work that goes on them. At the other extreme, we are becoming so dependent on commercial success, that it is quite hard if you believe in a new writer who is at odds with the current system. You can only really pursue and develop writers who show signs of commercial success. Another problem is that our theatre work lasts for only a very short time: You might have a wonderful production at The National Theatre and for a whole variety of reasons it just disappears in a year. I'm not saying we should have a production for 30 years but if an actor is greatly in demand, she or he won't commit himself or herself for many years. Because there's a big film to make or a big TV series. TV increasingly sucks actors and writers into it. You can earn so much more money as a writer writing a half-an-hour piece for a soap opera, than for a play that may take you half a year to work out properly. I don't know if we can find ways of restoring the equilibrium or not. We are excessively dependent on an economy that is out of balance.

KATE BASSETT:

Two strengths are that the U.K. still turns out excellent actors and a new wave of exciting young writers has recently emerged. One problem is that, because TV and film pay much better, the theatre loses actors and writers. Nevertheless, stage and screen feed one another. The theatre is a training ground. The screen makes people famous. Then, if they return to work in the theatre, that helps sell tickets (though I'm not a fan of star casting for the sake of it.)

Lottery money is now helping theatres improve their buildings enormously, though we have to mind we don't end up with more splendiferous buildings than fantastic productions. Of course, there's the continuing worry about the public – especially the younger generation – not going to the theatre in huge numbers. Then there's the fact that it's very expensive to put a show on in the West End, which means some seriously good plays which do not have mass appeal are not viable there. But then some really fine productions still make it into town – like Thelma Holt's production of Ibsen's *Doll's House*.

Also in terms of London, though it's not good for the capital to lose the RSC for half the year as the company heads into the regions, the Barbican is now free and is bringing in major international directors who will, doubtless, influence and thus add to British theatre's creativity.

MICHAEL BILLINGTON:

There's a kind of resilience in the British theatre in the face of economic deprivation. Subsidies have always been insufficient and yet British people go on year in, year out writing plays, directing and acting. The cornerstone of the British theatre is the quantity of living writers. Peter Hall used to say there are at least 30 first-rate living dramatists in Britain at any time. That's the thing that's kept me going as a theatre critic for 25 years. Generation after generation they seem to use theatre as a means of analysing the country and taking the moral temperature of the society. That goes back to Edward Bond, David Hare, Howard Brenton, David Edgar, Trevor Griffiths, and Howard Barker. In recent years there has emerged a new generation of interesting writers in their twenties with provocative, disillusioned plays about the state of Britain. We've also had successive generations of classic directors of high calibre in my lifetime and that has been sustaining – Peter Hall, John Barton, Trevor Nunn, Richard Eyre, Stephen Daldry, Katie Mitchell. The acting tradition is consistently strong as well. We seem to have the ability to produce extraordinarily good actors and that's a tradition that goes on from one generation to another.

The negative sides to British theatre at the moment are nearly all a product of economics rather than talent. It's the inhibiting effect of money that constricts us. It stops theatres from exploring a repertory as wide as they would like to. There are far too many adaptations of novels as opposed to new plays, particularly in regional theatres. Musicals have come to swamp the commercial theatres in a depressing way. They are a part of the theatrical spectrum but they've been elevated into a cultural statement, and they get a preposterous amount of attention and space in the papers. As if a new musical by Andrew Lloyd Webber is of a major significance to Western culture? I find the grant restrictions of drama schools depressing. The effect of that is that only the relatively well-off students can afford to go there. In about five years time we'll be paying the price of this. What's depressing me most is not the theatre but the attitude of the present conservative government to theatre and the arts – as if because we've somehow muddled through, we'll go on surviving indefinitely. There will come a point when that will no longer be true and people will say, "Why should I work for low wages in theatre when I can have more money in TV?" We already see the signs of that. I find the lack of permanent companies depressing as well.

JAMES CHRISTOPHER:

Probably our greatest strength is the subsidized theatre. If we didn't have The National Theatre and the RSC, we would drown in one or two-handed plays. These companies are the backbone of the theatre industry and everything else bounces off that. Another unique strength is the fringe. It came out of Edinburgh 25 years ago and made theatre sexy. The sheer quantity of it however is a problem. Some of it has become a theme park. But maybe you need a theme park so that everything else looks good beside it? If I had a choice I would close about half of the small theatres. I sometimes think that 70% of the people who put on a play should never be allowed near a stage. Unfortunately our stages are readily available to all these egos. There is no screening process. What little real quality there is tends to get diluted.

MICHAEL COVENEY:

The greatest strengths in the British theatre derive from a sense of community and common purpose in the profession despite all the factions and the severe economic constrains that are threatening its backbone: the regional theatres. I never cease to be amazed each week by the brilliance of our actors. Something in our national character – natural reserve, social inhibitions suspicion of flagrant behaviour – makes us very good actors. Also the love of language inculcated from the Celtic traditions gives us a real appreciation of good plays, good story-telling. It is important that the main institutions are preserved and renovated. Richard Eyre's reign at the Royal National Theatre has been exemplary, and he has restored almost single-handedly an idea of public service in the arts at a very important time. The BBC, for instance, the envy of the world, is expected to justify itself to politicians by competing commercially with other stations. And producers there are being disempowered by bureaucrats and marketing people. There are signs of this in the theatre and it is very dangerous. The Arts Council has at last admitted it was wrong to bully theatres into developing complicated marketing strategies and departments during the '80s. It is essential that public money goes to the work itself, not the beaurocrats; to the artist, not the apparatchik.

Hopefully a Labour government will recognize the importance of much more investment in the arts, but there are no signs yet. Still, the theatre survives, and there is the semblance of a new writing boom that has mostly emanated from Ireland and the Royal Court under Stephen Daldry that is immensely encouraging.

It is high time that more directors of Daldry's generation took on the running of theatres. One of the reasons Trevor Nunn has been appointed to succeed Richard Eyre at the National is that a whole generation decided to make its reputation by directing classics, not new plays, and refusing to go and run theatres in the regions. This has been very damaging. So there is not enough real talent now working outside of London. I would still love to see a network of "national" theatres, as in France, established in the major cities with vastly increased public subsidies. It is bad news that the Arts Council seems to support the Royal Shakespeare Company's campaign to tour the country a lot more, thereby disguising the terrible decline of theatre in the regions.

Another problem is arising in education. There is simply not enough money going to student grants, and not enough really good teaching of Shakespeare in schools or indeed, it appears, in drama schools. Actors acquire too little experience of big stage roles, because the regional theatres cannot afford to present large-cast classics any more, and their techniques are stunted by working in television.

NICK CURTIS:

The main problem is that there's too much theatre in London. I find it very difficult to stomach the complaints that there aren't enough plays going on when such an awful lot of bad plays are on at even the leading, subsidised theatres. I find it impossible to believe that there's somewhere a vast resource of brilliant playwrights, directors or actors who are starving. It's not enough to pump money into theatres to subsidize their existence. I'm not against subsidy but you can't purely throw money at the theatre to keep it going for its own sake. It has to be good enough to earn an audience.

At the moment the chief flaw in British theatre is a lack of quality control in the writing. We have no real dramaturgical tradition. Not enough work is being done on plays before they go into performance. It does happen in some places, obviously at The National Theatre, the RSC and in the independent new writing companies, but only there. Sometimes I'm quite astonished at the sort of things people believe are worth putting on stage. Part of the problem is that a lot of the playwrights are, maybe not consciously, using theatre as a step into TV or film and an awful lot of plays are TV plays which are being done on the stage. Or worse: radio plays. There's a failure to acknowledge that the theatre is not competing in the market place against other theatres but against other forms of entertainment. I always feel if I'm recommending a play, I have to be absolutely sure that I can say with a clean conscience to the reader, "If you go to see this, you'll have a better time than staying at home watching TV." Theatre has to concentrate on that which is theatrical. It doesn't always.

The strongest areas at the moment are what one could call the middle-band, which are the National Theatre, the RSC, and the other subsidized theatres – the Almeida, Hampstead, some of the art centres, the Bush, etc. We have writers who are still prepared to experiment. I don't know the

New York theatre scene but a number of American writers tell me they are no longer doing plots there. Whereas our theatre still tells stories. And interesting ones! That is good. Some of our actors are extremely good. We've still got a generation of tremendous older actors who are dedicated enough to continue working on stage for ludicrously small amounts of money on projects they believe in.

NICHOLAS DE JONGH:

The failure of the British theatre today relates to its entire history until 1968, being a censored theatre. From the 16th century on both Puritans, some of whom were not against drama, and non-Puritans recognized theatre's capacity to be subversive in a dissident way. It could potentially threaten the security of the realm, so theatre needed to be under surveillance and censorship. Now there's very little theatre, as opposed to TV, which makes news by dealing with life in a way that we find threatening, enraging, exciting, or even controversial. Theatre dramatists don't seem to address crucial modern or past issues in a way which seizes the headlines. That's a great failure today.

The positive has to do with the arrival of a generation of directors and scenic designers, who are not set upon social realism and who are so much involved at the Royal Court. An interesting and encouraging aspect is the departure from social realism into non-realistic, expressionistic modes of production and stage design. Richard Eyre and Adrian Noble are examples of the style, and Stephen Daldry is an obvious one.

JANE EDWARDS:

We have fantastic actors, directors, and designers. There is suddenly an enormous number of very young talented writers emerging, which is extremely exciting. Obviously money is a problem. I don't think the repertory system is going to recover. We need some new ideas. Most of all ticket prices need to come down. That's something the Lottery should address, otherwise the audience is going to get older and older. We've lost our companies altogether and that sense of trust and commitment that comes from working together over a long time. When the Maly Theatre came here from St. Petersburg, we saw the advantages of being a company. We have fantastic actors but we have a lot to learn from that training. The National Theatre building is a problem – both the Olivier and the Lyttleton are incredibly difficult to work in. The fact that we don't subsidize individuals but rather buildings is also a problem.

There's too much theatre in London. There's a new play taking off every three minutes and a lot of good things get lost. We are all rushing off to see different plays all the time. It's a sort of consumer-gobble-me-down-quick theatre culture. In Dublin, for instance, when a major play is done by the Abbey Theatre, the whole city goes to see it, so there's a sense of community sharing the experience. Just as happened at certain times in the past.

JOHN ELSOM:

There has been an astonishing flourishing of British writing. Some people would say this comes out as a result of subsidy. I'm skeptical about that because some of the best writers come through one of our commercial impresarios Michael Codron. He's promoted Joe Orton, Pinter, Gray, and Ayckbourn at a very early stage. This is one of the few countries in Europe where the commercial theatre means something. There's a number of good new playwrights these days. We also have a range of well-established writers whose work fills European and world theatres. It is astonishing that I go to Singapore and I find out that the only plays I can see there are British plays! … We have also a wonderful series of actors – generation after generation leaving drama schools – who are wonderfully competent. We've got some really remarkably competent directors as well.

What I find dissatisfying is the lack of seriousness in our theatre. Time and again I go to the theatre and find it not boring but brainless; it doesn't really leave me with any particular idea or insights. It's full of cliches. There's an anti-intellectualism in British theatre. I dislike it very much when people try to undermine the artist.

ROBERT GORE-LANGTON:

The great strength has been the sense of democracy within the production – that no one can take unique credit for the work. Theatre is a community event and I'm suspicious of theatre where one person in the production process is the star. I love punky design and I love European theatre with its direction and use of light and sound – all the sort of things that we often don't get here, but I think the idea of the guru in the theatre is a slightly depressing one. We have theatre leaders but they are generally not worshipped in the same way that they are abroad. We have a tradition of unflashy excellence on the stage, which I enjoy enormously. I like ensemble work. There are some wonderful foreign directors who come over and you think, "Christ! It's all happening somewhere else!" But it's easy to overlook what we've got.

Another strength is that we are blessed with an amazing acting community although it isn't really exploited.

The great failure has been that the theatre has lost its charisma. The reason is that so many writers, even extremely accomplished ones, defect to other media because the money's so bad. The writer who makes a living from the theatre is a dying breed and it's certainly dead in the commercial theatre. Unless there are enough people writing new work and producing new plays, the whole system will collapse. Another problem is that the West End is in a terrible state. But the failure comes largely from the economic climate: the producers are reluctant to put on anything interesting. The critics get used to see rubbish and start to think that there's good and bad rubbish. So we start to give two cheers to the better end of the market. That's a shame.

PETER HEPPLE:

The major strength of the British theatre is the great loyalty of the public to the theatre. There is an enormous demand for a live entertainment including theatre. If you came to London as a tourist you would expect to see a show. The average person will even go to a seaside resort like Scarborough and expect to see a show. Another strength is that there're a lot of people who want to be in the theatre. To a certain extent they are the people who have kept it going. This is why there are a thousand shows on the Edinburgh Fringe. The fact is that we are getting an enormous amount of fully trained actors, singers and dancers.

A problem is that a star-actor would not commit himself to a show for more than about 12 weeks. They do television series, films, or go to Broadway. The top of the profession have got more control over their careers than ever before because they make more money then ever before. It's a problem because we are so star-conscious ... The West End has a lot of problems. The prices are so high and for most people it's not worth it. Most people like me live outside of London and the transport difficulties you have to experience going to a West End theatre are not worth it. This has been to the advantage of theatres outside London – regional and provincial theatres and the most go-ahead impressarios have discovered this. I'd say that the strength of the British theatre is outside London.

IAN HERBERT:

The main weakness is, as always, the financial one. There just isn't enough money around to support the big, lavishly funded kind of theatre that many European cities will take for granted. Paradoxically, that weakness has produced strengths over the years – the strength and ingenuity of people conjuring money out of nowhere, or making projects happen even if there isn't a state subsidy to match. That has been very good. Another strength is the tons of new writers appearing now.

ROBERT HEWISON:

The strengths and weaknesses of the British theatre are very similar in the sense that it's very empirical, it's realistic, it lacks any great sense of the political, and it's aesthetically blind compared to the way the continental theatre is developing. Because theatre is actually so central to British culture, it reflects all the strengths and weaknesses of British culture in general. The good things are that it has managed to sustain itself over a very long period and it's still showing signs of energy and creativity. But I've felt over the last two or three years that some of that energy is beginning to drain away. Partially because there are more interesting things that are happening not in theatre as such. They are happening in galleries, in non-theatre spaces. That's where creativity or avant-garde is. British theatre is not really avant-garde, it's more middle-garde, if such a position exists. You only have to go to The National Theatre to see the English middle and upper class, really rejoicing in certain kinds of play.

JEREMY KINGSTON:

There was one time when I would have said "Well, theatre risks becoming a marginal activity." But in the same way that people have been turning back to the cinema recently against all forecast trends, I don't think that the theatre is in as bad a shape as it sometimes looks in the middle of a heat wave. It does have the most marvellous fund of capable actors and actresses. If there's a trouble ahead for the theatre, it's that so many young actors and playwrights go off and work on scripts for TV. One can see in plays, on the fringe or even in the West End, actors doing marvelous things and then you may not see them again because TV and films offer them more money and certainty. In the old phrase: you can make a killling from theatre but you can't make a living.

ALASTAIR MACAULAY:

The greatest virtue of the British theatre, for centuries, has been British acting. But some of its traditions are in danger of being forgotten in the pursuit of more sensationalist vocal or physical effects. I don't mean to knock some of the new acting styles, but it would be tragic if the tradition that produced Judi Dench and Maggie Smith did not go on to produce other exemplary stylists. The greatest acting is transparent.

Many people will say that the problem of our theatre today is money. But it's always been a hard time for money, and British theatre will muddle through, because it has a great deal of vitality. The real problems are larger cultural ones. I'm afraid it's nothing less than a decline in – a confusion about – our moral and social values.

SHERIDAN MORLEY:

One of the problems is that, apart from David Hare, we don't have political writers any more. I would have liked to have seen more plays in the last 10 years that worry about the state of the nation. During the last socialist government in the '60s, we had a huge number of playwrights who reflected the world around us and wrote plays about the miners' strike or industrial unrest. Now playwrights seem to have shied away from any state-of-the-nation plays and instead they are giving us a lot more sexual fantasy, urban terror, and feminism. They are influenced largely by the French and the American cinema. Actually most of them now seem to live in cinema rather than in the theatres. As a result we are in danger of copying the urban unrest Hollywood movies that are all over the place and we seem to have locked ourselves into certain areas which are very narrow.

We have a lot of plays out of Ireland which have been much better. We have been lately inclined to write only about single events and we have to learn from the Irish again that playwriting is about everybody: the way that Chekhov was writing about a small group of Russian aristocrats but everybody could find themselves somewhere in *Uncle Vanya* or *The Cherry Orchard*. That' s what we have to get back to – a state of generalized writing about the particular.

The strength of the British theatre is that we still have a very active theatre-going community who goes to the theatre as the Americans go to the movies. We go to the theatre very much more often that anywhere else in the world. Actually more people in this country go to the theatre than to football matches.

The problem with the West End is that now it has become a very expensive area where the ideal theatre-goers are the tourists because they by definition don't have a car, don't have children and are living in a hotel nearby, so all the problems the locals have – transport and money – are non-existent for them. Another problem is that the big musicals have now taken residence in about 15 theatres which means there is almost no movement. To produce a straight play on the West End now costs half a million pounds. So the costs are a real problem. Actors are more inclined to work on TV or radio, where the work is quicker, better paid and they can go back to their families at night.

Our fighting was all about permanent companies versus casuals, commercial theatre versus subsidized theatre, fringe theatres versus the blockbuster musicals. We have to have all of these. But at the moment the theatre is very volatile. If you have a difficult economic time, people become more conservative and inevitably that has an effect on the production so you find that the producers get more conservative. There are a lot of revivals around because they are familiar titles. If you can't afford a familiar star, then you have a familiar title and that at least gets the audience to buy tickets.

But I still think we are living in a very good theatre time, it's just that it's very unpredictable.

DAVID NATHAN:

We've got some wonderful actors and actresses, and some good new writers. Although some of the plays that have been praised by almost everybody are rather sloppy. For instance, most people say that *Mojo* is a wonderful play. I didn't like it not because I didn't like the force of the writing but because I thought it was untrue to the '50s. The answer I got was, "Oh, well, the playwright wasn't alive in those days." That's no answer. If you write a play about Napoleon, you don't make him six-foot tall because you weren't alive in those days. The tendency to overpraise new writing is not good because the writer will think that he has already accomplished far more than in fact he has. Or she has.

There is also a lack of good commercial product. The nationally subsidized theatres like The National Theatre and RSC on the whole are doing pretty well, especially The National ... And there is a wonderful wave of new writing, particularly Jewish writing, headed by the Royal Court.

BENEDICT NIGHTINGALE:

The West End is in a rather worrying state. There seems to be a lack of adventurousness. It does face many of the same problems as Broadway does. There are an awful lot of cabaret-compendium shows. It's quite difficult to get serious straight plays. The audiences seem to be staying away from them. Therefore producers are not taking risks. Costs and seat prices are going up.

The rest of the London theatre is in a lively state. There is a feeling again that theatre's the place to be at. There's some sense of adventure around. We've got a very lively set of directors. There's a wave of quite interesting young playwrights suddenly appearing out of nowhere. So it's such a complicated situation: on the one hand, you have West End which seems to be a dilapidated place and, on the other hand, you have bits of the fringe and bits of the national theatre circuit that are lively.

Another thing that we've had to come to terms with recently – with which I certainly have problems and don't know quite what to do about – is the emergence of performance art more into the mainstream. People like Theatre de Complicite are moving more into metaphor and against realism. At what point is this creative and helpful and at what point does it become self-indulgent and showy – art for art's sake? In the early '90s I used to feel that I was seeing very elaborate, clever sets which were making amazingly brilliant comments on the play, and in a way had highjacked the play ... Quite often I feel that we are not interested in foreign work as much as we should be. One of the dangers with the British theatre is that we tend to be slightly self-satisfied. Everyone says, "Oh, the British theatre is the best in the world!" We can say that in comparison with the American theatre, but can we say that when we really keep very thinly abreast with the European theatre?

JOHN PETER:

It is becoming more and more difficult unless your parents have money to go to a drama school. In the long term, unless something is done about this quickly, this is going to restrict the quality of actors. I also worry that too many young actors, who come out of drama schools, are not good speakers and they think that impersonation is enough. It is not enough.

One of the strengths of the British theatre is that British directors and actors are much more flexible in their tastes than directors and actors on the continent, and are willing to be in most kinds of plays unless they think the play is bad. Another strength is that there is much more contact between generations. Great actors are more approachable to young actors. The setting of an example is much more first-hand than on the continent, and this is reflected in the quality of the supporting actors.

IAN SHUTTLEWORTH:

The weaknesses are the economic climate and the timidity of producers to use what resources they have to the maximum. One of the strengths is precisely the opposite of that: those producers who do explore the limited resources to the maximum. Another strength is the growing sense of non-willingness of young writers to be bound by notions of propriety. They know the effect they want to achieve and know how to deploy shock with precision rather than just splattering about.

CHARLES SPENCER:

It sounds chauvinistic but I think theatre in Britain is the best in the world and we have the finest actors in the world, particularly for classical plays. Another thing, of course, that Britain has got, that the other countries haven't got, is Shakespeare and all these other dramatists, and a great tradition of doing theatre. One of the things I like about the job is that you see about 30 Shakespeare productions a year. It keeps you in touch with what matters about the human heart. The diversity of the British theatre is another strength. There used to be many complaints in the '60s and '70s that British actors could only act from their neck up. That's not true now. There are companies like Théâtre de Complicité and the physical theatre is playing an increasing part. In fact I'm getting slightly tired by it now. It's becoming a cliché.

As far as the West End goes, there isn't as much serious work there as 30 years ago. But if the West End was all there was about British theatre, then it would be in a very parlous state. However 30 years ago there wasn't the National Theatre, there wasn't the RSC, and there wasn't the fringe with the terrific boom in new writing. There may well be a decline in the West End with the young audience largely because it's very expensive, there's no evidence of decline among the fringe theatres. There's a lot of theatre outside London as well.

But there's one real danger at the moment: the most talented young playwrights tend to get snapped up by TV and film because the money is better. In the old days what kept people going was that the straight plays would be transferred from a theatre like Hampstead or The Bush to the West End where they'd be earning 10% of the gross, which is a lot of money. The straight plays are not tending to run in the West End anymore. So these very talented playwrights haven't got the chance to earn big money in the theatre, like Stoppard and Ayckbourn did 10–20 years ago. It will be interesting to see how many of today's bright young things will be still writing for the theatre 10 years from now.

JACK TINKER:

One of the problems is that our theatre has to rely more and more on sponsorship. That's tedious because people only want to sponsor what is safe. Writers have to be allowed to be heard. They can only know if a play is good or bad when it is on the stage. If they can't get their plays seen as well as read, they are never going to develop their craft.

Having said that, I'm amazed by the amount of new writing talent that is still coming to the front line. We have some very far-sighted producers too who do try to encourage it. The West End has become a much healthier mix because it can afford to constantly be generating new productions that are going to both fill the theatre and be exciting drama, not just boring old favorites because they bring money. Commercial producers are relying more and more on subsidized theatres to generate new writing and then are working in a partnership with the West End. This is giving a whole new look to the West End.

The bad thing is that the British theatre is far too inward-looking. We sometimes see a new Romanian theatre and they show such a standard of ensemble acting! Even at the RSC they don't get that standard.

IRVING WARDLE:

Our theatre is going through times that nobody really approves of very much. The Royal Court of the '50s and '60s was to me what theatre was really for. It was a sounding board radiating out far beyond the audience that went to the theatre. The work you went to see there was a kind of statement about the English life. I don't know why but that doesn't happen now. I seldom have the feeling of really participating in something that is absolutely necessary as one used to get with Osborne, Pinter, and with directors like Peter Brook.

MATT WOLF:

One real strength of the British theatre is the quality of the audience. In America you tend to get the buzz, but the down-side is that people go only if there is a buzz because they actually want to say at the drinks party they'll be at next Friday that they saw so and so. Here they go to *John Gabriel Borkmann* because they want to see Paul Scofield, or they like Ibsen, or Richard Eyre. And they listen much better. There's a quality of active attention and real active participation in theatre. TV has dulled audiences in the States a lot. Having said that, I think that probably there's too much theatre here for the audience to be able to see it. And probably for the audience that wants to see it.

2

BRITISH THEATRE TODAY: THE THEATRE-MAKERS' REPORT

Playwrights:

Sir Alan Ayckbourn
Steven Berkoff
David Edgar
Arnold Wesker

Directors:

Howard Davies
Sir Richard Eyre
David Farr
Sir Peter Hall
Jonathan Kent
Nicolas Kent
Sam Mendes
Katie Mitchell
Adrian Noble
Trevor Nunn
Max Stafford-Clark

Producers:

Thelma Holt
Sir Cameron Mackintosh
Michael Morris
Tom Morris
Peter Wilkins

Press-Agents and a Publisher:

Martin Coveney
Sue Hyman
Nick Hern
Sharon Kean
Sue Rolfe

They answer the questions:

– What are the main strengths and weaknesses of the contemporary British theatre? What are the problems it faces today?

SIR ALAN AYCKBOURN:

The obvious problem is the lack of serious financial investment. Certainly regionally. British theatre is slowly being strangled through lack of money from central government, which is ultimately where all subsidy comes from. Throughout my life time, government has traditionally been the patron ever since the enlightened creation of a national Arts Council after the war. My work would not have existed but for the subsidized theatre. It all started here – at the Stephen Joseph Theatre. It was money invested with tremendous care. Not just for one play, that's the point. Because if you run a theatre and you adopt a dramatist, you take on a long-term commitment to them far beyond one play. That problem is, that long term patronage is getting more and more difficult to come by and that is a problem not just for us here but nationally. Once you stop that process you rely on one-off successes. On dramatists who miraculously manage the trick once and then spend the rest of their lives wondering how they did it. Or on revivals.

It's been apparent in the last two decades when we've had few major dramatists brought forward. We've had major plays but no major dramatists. The ones people who run theatres like this can turn to when the going gets tough. Dramatists you can rely on to help with the rent. In other words, ones who can fill a theatre. My preoccupation at present is to re-establish that sort of playwright who can both challenge and question and yet still entertain. I want a new generation of writers to get the chance to explore what theatre can do. What can be achieved through the manipulation of time and space for instance. Or what the potential of an actor truly is if your writing can only release it. Refusing to explore theatre, claiming that content is absolutely everything, is like a painter refusing to open his paint-box in case the colours get in the way of the picture. Stephen Joseph, my mentor, once said to me, "Write a well-made play or two first." "I don't want to write well-made plays," I replied, "I want to write plays that shatter conventions not perpetuate them." He insisted, "At present, you are like a monkey with a typewriter. Trying to break the rules before you've even discovered what they are. First discover them; then you'll know when you're breaking them. And why."

Many new playwrights are writing movie script, not stage plays at all. That's fine, but why send them to the theatre? Could it be because they don't in truth know the difference?

STEVEN BERKOFF:

Funding has much less to do with the problems of British theatre than they think. A lot of people talk about it because in a way it's like men who talk about sex. It's a mask, a way of dealing with your lack of art or creative insight. If you don't have that, you fall back on funding because it's a substitute. As it is, theatre *is* funded. Any funding that comes free is fantastic, and nothing should be obligatory, as if it is your wife. Most of the theatres get well-funded, but there is a tendency that people have little to say. Because funding is like loo paper in the loo. It's necessary but the more funding doesn't increase your artistic creativity. It's like the alcoholic chasing the first drink: if he gets more, he suddenly will get better, then he gets worse.

Every theatre has its own problems, like a different family. The main problem is the lack of vision, ideology and insight, the lack of uniting the disparate parts of society. The theatre is still an elitist small group controlled by a few people. There is no embracing working class culture. There are no great dramas coming out of the working class culture as there were 40 years ago. Neither is the theatre absorbing physical skills. There's a hot-house environment: the same names go backwards and forwards, you see the same boring directors and the same work over and over again. These directors may be worthy people and they have to work, but I wouldn't want to see the same six authors. It's a bit of a club and they have a season ticket from the RSC to The National and back again. Years ago I could see directors from France, Germany, Israel, Russia. There was a far greater freedom. When Laurence Olivier ran The National Theatre, there was a far more intensive theatre. He invited the Berliner Ensemble, for example. Through them, through him, through Kenneth Tynan I was able to see great actors and directors like Bergman, Zeffirelli, and Brecht. Now the major companies have no interest in internationalism. I want to see big names, interesting people, extraordinary directors from America or France. I never see that anymore. It means that the public is cheated for their tax-pounds. That means that our theatres don't have any personality. I think every theatre should be different. Like the way The Théâtre National Populaire is different from Comédie Française and that in turn is different from some other theatre in Paris. The actors here are very good. But apart from that I'd say there is little good in British theatre. Nothing innovative. There is little reason to go to it: it's a depressing experience, it's defunct, it's non-productive in a sense that it doesn't sow seeds that influence young groups and other people. It slavishly repeats what it's done the year before. They still insist on having revolving stages and sets even at The Globe! When Shakespeare begged the audience to "piece out our imperfections with your thoughts", I thought the whole point was there were to be no sets. There's a kind of worshipping of the director. I have seen one or two individual directors who have impressed me. But the only production with an extraordinary power that I've seen in the last 10 years is *The Inspector Calls*. The rest is silence or mistakes.

MARTIN COVENEY:

It's a public opinion that British theatre is the best theatre in the world. But it's receiving less and less support from the government in terms of subsidy. That affects especially the provincial theatre which is a great strength of British theatre.

HOWARD DAVIES:

The strength is that we have government subsidy. It's been savagely eroded over the years to the point where people are struggling to survive and theatres go to the wall. But, at places like the RSC and The National Theatre, we still have the privilege to work on pieces for 6 or 7 weeks of rehearsal, we can still afford to get top actors and take the risk with classical or controversial plays with big casts of over 20. Also, there is a kind of an acknowledgement of the classics even if we play with it and sometimes abuse it. That gives our actors a cross-reference and some cultural muscle. That gives them a sense of what language can do on the stage – that through language you can come very close to expressing emotions, ideas and your own doubts. That is a huge strength. The weakness is that we have lost our political will to believe in theatre. We apologize, we believe that if hospitals are going short of funds, then how could we possibly claim the right to be artists working with a government subsidy, how dare we put ourselves forward?! We don't have the courage to argue our corner – to see ourselves as part of the cultural environment of this country.

DAVID EDGAR:

The accessibility of the British theatre and its willingness to listen to the audience is its main strength and its weakness.... A very good thing is that over the last two or three years there's been a lot of really exciting new work by young writers, for the first time in 10 or 15 years. There's a whole new generation of playwrights in their twenties writing excitingly about today. Everybody is talking about the great cultural revival in Britain and, in the theatre, that's what they are talking about. They are not talking about productions of *Uncle Vanya*, they are talking about those young writers. They perform in the Theatre Upstairs and you can't get in to see them, they are so popular. But my fear is that in 10 years time the small-scale theatre won't be thriving. It's a fear because I think the strength of British theatre has been in the relationship between its various branches ...

The other thing in Britain is that because the TV is now dominated by police or hospital series, and there is so little one-off TV drama, theatre has

moved into this area and many of the new plays are what could have been
TV plays.

SIR RICHARD EYRE:

The humanity is the main strength of our theatre. The point of the medium
is the relationship between an individual or a group of individuals on stage
and a group of individuals in the audience. Everything in the theatre is
about relationships. It's also about human scales. You are always committed
to the scale of the human body and voice. Any theatre which tries to defy
that, and a lot of German theatres do, takes away the essence of what theatre
is. British theatre is thoroughly and damagingly pragmatic but it's finally
humane. I remember taking a production to Hamburg and a review saying
that the show was revolutionary in the context of German theatre because
it put such an emphasis on the actors' performance. I thought, "What else
is there in the theatre?" We are stuck up with the human being.

The problem of the theatre is always one: imagination. You could say it's
money but to some extent all you could do with money is create conditions
in which talent could flourish and emerge, and you can hope it appears.
You can't legislate for talent appearing, you can't manufacture it. There's
an element of ... call it *luck* or *destiny* ... I would like to see funding theatre in
this country increased – not hugely but to an extent that we could get rid of
the constant arguing about money. I would like to see the whole educational
system change so that it changed the view of culture and it was less class
based.

DAVID FARR:

The major strength is the incredible enthusiasm on the ground roots level.
A number of people work on tiny productions all over London and all over
other cities. That's probably unparalleled anywhere else. And it's incredible
that people still carry on given the astonishing lack of money. We're also in
a relatively strong position as far as new writing is concerned. We should
be very proud of that. But on the whole our theatre is in a confused state at
the moment. On the one hand, we still have the remnants of a rather beautiful
English style of theatre – the great spoken theatre. On the other hand, there
is the increasing influence of Europe – the visual theatre, the use of ensemble
casts, the director being a tyrant. So there's an interesting mixture. What
comes out of that at the end is, at its worst, the RSC – a strange old-fashioned
bureaucracy producing rubbish on a daily basis. It's basically like going to
the Tower of London. On the good side, there are the independent companies
like Théâtre de Complicité and Cheek by Jowl who are doing interesting

work. I also still think that a lot of good work is done at The National Theatre. That's one of the things I'm most impressed by: how our National Theatre manages to still produce work of integrity, interest and honesty. The independent companies are amazing too. The Gate Theatre is, of course, my favorite one, but the Bush Theatre and the Royal Court are also exciting, and I'm sure there are others. I don't know too many outside London.

The main problem is largely in the West End which doesn't seem to work very well except for the five or six musicals that really do work. The Andrew Lloyd Webber thing is perfectly justifiable on the level of business. It's like selling golf balls. It's not theatre but it makes money and that's fine. If you have a great time, there's nothing wrong with it. It's terrible when people attack it. But when you're being subsidized, you have a responsibility not to use that money for an excuse to make more money. Like the RSC. You have a responsibility to try and produce thoughtful work, to elevate people's ideas, and to produce work that is contemporary. And not to sell a show as a piece of entertainment with a slight veneer of art on the top. In the end the biggest problem is simply – do you really believe that in 50 years people will still be going to the theatre? I hope so.

SIR PETER HALL:

I'm optimistic about the theatre because there's a lot of talented new writing. There are a huge number of new writers under 30. This is surprising and wonderful. But the previous Conservative government has weakened the theatre as it has weakened our broadcasting. They've given broadcasting to Rupert Murdoch and they've given the theatre to tourists. They haven't supported the regional theatre, which is where talent is and the new audiences are. That's tragic. But the English have a great capacity to invent things and destroy them. We created the most extraordinary theatre culture in history in the time of Shakespeare and a few years later we completely destroyed it. We are quite capable of re-inventing it all.... The major weakness is the apathy of public. They don't yell at their politicians to look after what we do so well. But there you are, you can't tell the public what to do ... I do believe that if it were not for the subsidized theatre, theatre would be as dead here as it is in America.

NICK HERN:

I'm sure everybody says *money* is the main problem but I think there's something more significant than money. It's a sense of will and a sense of making a contribution. Theatre is not regarded as very important. It's been sliding down the list of social and cultural priorities. So the theatre itself understandably becomes more inward-looking, more tentative and embattled. What one would like for it is a new dose of optimism, as in the mid '50s. Every now and again there's a combination of circumstances which makes you feel, "Oh God, yes, that's wonderful! There really is nothing to beat a good night in the theatre." One good night can make you forgive the last 15 or 16 times when you've just had a completely bad experience. So if I had a wish I'd wish it courage and heart almost more than money. Because if you've got the courage and heart, the money will follow.

Another problem is that theatre is divided into a series of ghettos. On the one hand, there are the West End theatres and the last few regional reps which still are patronized by a very tiny portion of the population. They are more to do with going out than going to the theatre. At the other end of the scale, going to The Bush or the Theatre Upstairs is an extraordinary experience, but simply isn't for everybody either. So it's not a more democratic form of theatre, it's just *another* form of theatre.

As for strengths, there are some very, very good actors and one or two very good directors. But there are too many not-good directors. That's a problem. Directors are insufficiently trained, and the good ones become good almost by accident. Writers too are very variable, but again there is no forum in which they can watch and learn from their fellows. It remains a very isolated, hit-and-miss profession.

THELMA HOLT:

Most of the problems we face are due to our economic situation and our inability to grapple with it properly. Our young are not given the opportunities required to secure the stability of our theatre for tomorrow. Our repertory system is eroded, and there is nowhere to hone your craft. There is also no automatic system for mandatory grants for students of either dance or drama. This is disastrous. Our weakness lies in the fact that we are not shoring up the quality of tomorrow. Our strength lies in our raw talent, which is second to none.

SUE HYMAN:

We have the best actors – that's the main strength. The weakness is that people don't want to take the risk of putting on a new play.

SHARON KEAN:

Theatre is underestimated as a British product – something which brings people to Britain to spend money on. The problem is that a lot of individuals subsidize the theatre. We've all done it: everybody goes through a phase when they're young and work for virtually nothing. Those people are actually subsidizing the theatre. They can't afford a car, a home, and children because they are doing that. That's something that the government exploits. It says – we don't need to give funding because they obviously can carry on.

JONATHAN KENT:

Our theatre is going through some sort of a crisis. There's too much theatre. Well, another way of putting that is: there's not enough good theatre, there's too much mediocre theatre. British theatre is ill-defined at the moment. In the '60s, certainly, in the '70s and the beginning of the '80s, theatre and new writing was seen as an instrument of social change. This is something I've never believed in. I don't believe theatre is a direct instrument of social change. It's an arena for emotional and spiritual expression which in turn can lead to social change, but to be used simply as a form of a didactic agitprop is a mistake. But I think theatre is beginning to find its role – especially in a society which at present is going through such an extraordinary sea-change. The qualities that theatre can offer – the quickening of the spirit, the enlivening of the heart and mind – are qualities, which at the end of the 20th Century, this country seems now able to accept and celebrate.

NICOLAS KENT:

Money is a huge problem. Now with the Lottery money we're refurbishing theatres and having these wonderful buildings but they have nothing to do with an audience. Because we're not allowed to spend money on actors and creative things. The more money you spend on theatres, the more you make theatre happen only in the theatres, which isn't necessarily the right way. Often you get a company of brilliant actors who find some space and they make it work for them. If you keep on pouring money into making theatres beautiful, in the end you're subsidizing buildings and the art that happens in them is secondary. It's more important to keep the artists alive.

The strength is that we're still a writer-based theatre. We believe in writers. I hope the other strength is that we believe in communication. But I'm beginning to think more and more that our theatre is becoming inward looking and that is the biggest danger. Actors are doing things because they want to show-case their talent rather than trying to find a method of communicating something to an audience. Directors are doing that as well. We have also become terribly design-based to the extent that designers are often in contradiction with the actors. I believe very strongly that in the theatre the actor comes first, the writer comes second, and the director comes a very late third. Now we are employing fewer actors because there is less money and we aren't putting enough emphasis on their skills, we aren't giving them a chance to try things and work in repertory theatre.

SIR CAMERON MACKINTOSH:

The British musical theatre is again going through one of its less-inspired patches at the moment. There's not really enough original work. Plays are doing better than musicals but you don't have the feeling of fantastic creativity anywhere. However, it's just one of those cycles that the profession goes through. All countries go through different patterns. Britain has had 15 years of tremendous creativity whilst in America, with the single exception of Stephen Sondheim, musical theatre has been through a 25-year uninspired patch. Now it's coming out of it and you're starting to see sprouts of new talent. I'm sure once again the American musical theatre will regain its position at the forefront of musical production. In the end it doesn't matter where musicals come from as long as they are good. London and New York will always be the main source of this particular kind of creation but now that the love of musicals is a world wide phenomenon I'm sure new writers will appear in all corners of the globe.

SAM MENDES:

The main problem is the total lack of money.

Outside that, you could say there is a much flatter theatre landscape now than there used to be. In the early '60s, there were a large number of differing schools of theatre and differing aesthetics: Olivier beginning the National Theatre in Chichester, Peter Hall and Trevor Nunn at the RSC, John Neville at Nottingham Playhouse, George Devine at the Royal Court etc., etc. Now many theatres in London are very similar. Many of the same people work in them and as a consequence the aesthetics of all those theatres become merged. On the one hand, this makes for a very supportive and friendly environment, on the other hand, there is something about enmity that is creative: aesthetics are often formed in relation to other people's beliefs.

Also, there are many artists who are not a part of the community of people who work in those places. Particularly writers like Arnold Wesker and Edward Bond, writers who don't deserve to be marginalized. They should surely be given some sort of platform despite the fact that they are complex and opinionated people. In the present climate they have no home.

KATIE MITCHELL:

I don't know because I don't go and see enough. I work so hard: I do three shows a year. I might be lucky enough to go to the theatre a maximum of 10 times a year, and that's not enough to answer such a question. It's more interesting to sometimes sit in the tube and see what's going around: someone to be kind to you or to sit next to someone who is mentally ill. There are so many other things to do: to listen to music or see the visual arts, or travel. There're so many things that fuel theatre. If you go only to the theatre, there's a danger that you'll become only influenced by other bits of theatre and they don't necessarily reflect what's going on in the community outside, which is after all who you are actually making your work for.

MICHAEL MORRIS:

British theatre is restrained because of the literary and naturalistic traditions in England. We've always thought of theatre as being literary. Even Shakespeare is studied in literary terms. I find that strange because Shakespeare has nothing to do with literature. He is about theatre and non-naturalistic theatre at that. Things are slowly beginning to change now: the visual element, which is so important in other parts of the world, is starting to be important in our theatre too. Design, sound, light, and other elements are being taken more seriously, as an integral part of the mise-en-scène.

In my view naturalism is no longer a medium for the theatre. It's done best on TV. That's where it belongs. Yet so much theatre in Britain is burdened with naturalism. We have a large predominance of TV plays in our theatres.

One of the strengths in English theatre is the acting and there also some interesting writers. Audiences are another strength too. They can be very discerning. They are the best critic.

TOM MORRIS:

British theatre is in a massive state of change at the moment. It is basically the result of money from the National Lottery. It is only just beginning to have its effect. A lot of what is interesting about British theatre has been created through improvisation in spaces which are not built for theatre. There's a kind of danger when we have all this money, that suddenly we will build lots of new, wonderfully equipped theatres but we might lose that gift of improvisation. For me it's very important that some of that money goes into a different kind of support which enables the next generation to make their work in strange places outside the new theatres which will be there.

I don't know any bad things about British theatre. There are a lot of things that I don't want to do here, at BAC. I don't like basically screenplays put on stage but it happens all over the place and I can't deny it's very popular. What I want here is a different kind of theatre. Theatre of imagination.

ADRIAN NOBLE:

The great strength of the British theatre is that it has consistently managed to combine the intellectual high ground and the common taste. Another strength is the power of the actor: the actors are more powerful here than anywhere else in the world. Often that comes for the directors as well ... There are a lot of weaknesses that are not essential. They are caused by the factor that regional theatres have been drained of resources and therefore their infrastructure has been seriously weakened. That's why you get the very talented people go to TV. But they don't rehearse in TV: you work for five minutes and you shoot. That goes hand in hand with the career pressures that actors are now under in this country. Also, there's a shift of the public taste created by the great musicals. if you talk to student directors or designers, they don't want to design or direct plays – they want to design and direct events.

TREVOR NUNN:

Politicians often stand up and say, "We can congratulate ourselves that OUR theatre in Britain is the best theatre in the world. It has great diversity. It has influential new writing. The performers tend to quite often end up as movie stars, to be awarded for Oscars and so on." That's fine in the sense that politicians need to be able to say that their subsidy is well spent, that the Lottery and the Arts Council really do a great deal of good. Obviously they do but it's dangerous for anybody to start to believe their own publicity. It's dangerous for the British theatre to do that ... One of the problems is the extreme financial deprivation in the regional theatres right across the land. The Arts Council allocation gets reduced each year and the government has also imposed rate capping, so that local councils have to make do with a smaller sum of money. In so many communities the council has decided that they can first of all dispense with giving a grant to the theatre. Therefore very little work is now arriving from the regions into West End where previously there was a constant flow of rigorous and daring projects. Neither are we sufficiently influenced and inspired by theatre companies from elsewhere. There used to be The World Theatre Seasons at the Aldwych Theatre every year presented under the banner of the RSC. Not only were the practitioners influenced by productions of the Moscow Art Theatre or The Berliner Ensemble. Not only did they have their eyes opened and felt they were in receipt of all sorts of new challenges, but audiences too would discover that there were other ways of looking at things and higher expectations that they could have that were not necessarily being fulfilled by work in this country. Visiting productions have come to The National Theatre from time to time but there's never been a main-stage season again. There's the LIFT season, which is excellent. It's something that deserves everybody's support. I'm passionately interested that more such work should happen. Exchange in every way should happen. Particularly at the speed we are heading towards Europe, the exchange and cross-checking of the work that goes on in the different European countries is very important. I personally believe in forging a better relationship with America too.

There's also the issue of the social revolution which is attached to the Internet and the possibilities of cyberspace, and each individual having a relationship with their own screen. The live and collective experience is beginning to have less significance in people's lives. Once we've become aware of that, it'll be relatively easy to target that as a problem and find the ways of getting people to go to a live performance in the theatre in clear contrast from the small screen experience. For 50 years people have been predicting that technological entertainment is going to wipe out the theatre. Possibly it will. But I would have thought that the theatre has done well in resisting those challenges.

SUE ROLFE:

The strength is that there are still new generations who come up and fight against what is going on in the mainstream. The weaknesses are, as they always were, in the West End. Producers lack imagination to change the taste of the public and to encompass the things that have been achieved on the fringe. If they had the guts to take the risk, they would probably find all these new things very much embraced by new generations. The main problem of the British theatre has to do with finance. 20 years ago it had the almost same problem but it wasn't so overwhelmed by it. It was easier to mount a production knowing that you had no money and because you weren't expecting any money, they did better and more exciting work. Now everybody's led to expect money. Also: before there weren't administrators at the level we have them now. They are extremely damaging to the whole fabric of the theatre.

MAX STAFFORD-CLARK:

The major problem for the British theatre is subsidy. Subsidy plus talent equals genius. Without subsidy it's hard to create genius. But on the whole there's a lot more to be proud of than there is to be worried about. There's a generation of young directors, just as there is a generation of young writers who are terrific. The standard of British design and direction has gone up enormously over the last 10 years. People would say that British theatre is insular. Well, we are not aware enough of what is happening on the Continent, in Australia, and in Canada. However, we are always aware of what's going on in America. Moreover: on the whole American theatre is dominated by the English theatre. American writers, like Tony Kushner, look to, and are inspired by, the English model. But I would wish we had more contacts with our fellow Europeans.

ARNOLD WESKER:

There's a lot of good and intelligent writing in England that has a certain power and passion but it doesn't take off. There are interesting individual plays rather than interesting writers. For example, I'm not terribly touched by David Hare's plays, but he did write one extraordinary play – *Plenty*, which was everything that he's tried to do since. I'm not a Pinter fan, but *The Caretaker* and *The Birthday Party* are plays which stand out. Trevor Griffiths wrote *Comedians* – a wonderful play! And one of the best plays of the last 20 years is *The Steward of Christendom* by Sebastian Barry.

We have wonderful actors. The drama schools are pouring out stunning young actors but there are fewer and fewer places for them to work. When I was directing one of my plays in Stockholm, I kept saying to the actors, "Let the lines work themselves. You don't have to act dramatically lines which have drama within them." After a while they said, "We know what you mean. English actors are very good at it, we are not."

The worst things about British theatre are the administration and funding. We produce some of the best theatre in the world and I don't know how we do it with such a little funding. It could be greater and more extensive if there was more support. Another unhealthy trend is the widening gap between the writer, on the hand, and the director and theatre administrator, on the other. The theatre is entirely in the charge of the director and it's humiliating. I'd like to be in a position of saying "No" to a director rather than having directors saying "No" to me. This has led to a kind of rudeness and ugliness of relationships. When John Osborn was given an award for his contribution to the English theatre, he said in his thank-you speech,

"This is an awful profession!" And he touched the nerve! In a letter to me, written June 1993, he observed: " ... It is accepted that writers are treated like shit." There's an ugliness creeping into the theatre that is disturbing.

PETER WILKINS:

The commercial theatre is facing a crisis and nobody quite knows why the crisis is coming upon us. It's rather like a rolling dust cloud and we're feeling the early effects of it. People are not coming to the theatre in the number that they used to in the past. Clearly we are not putting on what they want to see. But what they want to see isn't quite clear. For one thing, people have to be pretty certain they'll get value for their money and that's what perhaps we're not delivering. The big musicals are scoring because people do come out and say, "Well, we didn't like it all that much but we did see some spectacle!" Perhaps if our plays were more thought-provoking, people would come out and say, "Well, my Lord, that gave us something to think about."

Part VI
Remembrance Of Time Wasted

1

WHEN CRITICS DECIDE THEY SHOULD HAVE WATCHED TV

Paul Allen	Robert Hewison
Kate Bassett	Jeremy Kingston
Michael Billington	Alastair Macaulay
James Christopher	Sheridan Morley
Michael Coveney	David Nathan
Nick Curtis	Benedict Nightingale
Nicholas de Jongh	John Peter
Jane Edwards	Ian Shuttleworth
Robert Gore-Langton	Charles Spencer
John Gross	Jack Tinker
Bill Hagerty	Irving Wardle
Ian Herbert	Matt Wolf

They answer the question:

– *What is a waste of time in the theatre for you?*

PAUL ALLEN:

It's a waste of time when I find no real surprises, no emotion, no jokes that I haven't seen in theatre before. It's a waste of time to see something I could have predicted before I went in. Even when the only purpose of theatre is to entertain, it has to open up something that's unexpected. There are evenings in which I think, "I shouldn't have gone to the theatre. I should have gone to the pub and had an interesting conversation instead."

KATE BASSETT:

Bad acting; dim directing; they wreck and obscure many a decent play. Sugary sentimentality, though I can stomach a bit of this if the show has bounce. Biographical rock musicals where they've made a complete dog's dinner of the story line and the songs sound better at home on your stereo. Lastly, of course, there's queueing for the entire interval in the Ladies.

MICHAEL BILLINGTON:

Sitting through anything to which one is temperamentally unsuited. My increasing answer to that is not to go in the first place. I'm old enough to guess what I'm going to be bored by or fed up with, and therefore not keen to attend. I stay away from a lot of things that a lot of my colleagues go to. I stay away from adaptations of novels and from a lot of musicals these days. It doesn't take too much intelligence to guess whether the musical is going to work or not.

JAMES CHRISTOPHER:

Revivals and mediocre shows. Companies should be encouraged not to keep on digging up old plays. They often do it because the director wants to be clever and put a topical spin on an old chestnut. But there are far too many topical spins on far too many old chestnuts. It becomes a mere exercise. I also find it infuriating when people use theatre space as a showcase for their underwhelming talents, or as an application for the RSC.

MICHAEL COVENEY:

Very little. Michael Billington might say novel adaptation. I don't know. I even quite like bad things.

NICK CURTIS:

Radio and TV plays on stage. People who think that just because *they* feel something that's enough reason to put it on stage. Indulgence is what I detest most in both writers, actors, and critics. There is a fantastic definition by Michael Blakemore. I interviewed him once and he said, "I loathe pretension and I refuse to be bored." That mirrors my attitude to the theatre.

NICHOLAS DE JONGH:

The theatre has an infinite capacity to surprise. I go in sometimes expecting to dislike something hugely and find myself disarmed by it. Similarly, when I expect to be quite interested by something, I'm not. Beyond that I'd say time-wasting theatre is contrived, insincere, expected, predictable, mundane, obvious, complacent, cozy, reliable, familiar. All these things tend to make me think, "Oh, yes. Not again!"

JANE EDWARDS:

Something that sets out merely to be entertaining and isn't.

ROBERT GORE-LANGTON:

What upsets me most is going to a show that has no apparent reason as to why it's been done – it's just another play because the theatre needs to put on another play. There has to be an imperative behind a thing being put on. Somebody's got to believe in the need to do it.

JOHN GROSS:

A bad commercial play is obviously boring, but a production of a great play by Molière, Chekhov or Shakespeare from which I get nothing is even worse. Because with the greatest playwrights you always ought to get something in principle. Even a mediocre production reminds you of the play. If I see inferior acting or an unsuccessful experimental play by a young writer – never mind. But a production from one of our leading companies which deliberately distorts a great play – well, that's another matter, and something which makes me impatient.

BILL HAGERTY:

You go and see a really bad film and you feel you've wasted your time. But with theatre very rarely do I come away without having found something in it that was at the very least interesting. Not necessarily very good, but interesting. Even in a bad play with a really bad director – the performance might be good. In Edinburgh, on the Festival Fringe, you can see some terrible stuff and you come out thinking, "Well, that was interesting!" You hated it, but it had something to hold the attention. So very rarely would I say it was a wasted evening.

IAN HERBERT:

I don't often waste my time in the theatre – if I find I'm wasting my time, I just go to sleep. It's an easy way out. The nearest thing to a waste of time is watching a group that thinks it's discovered a brilliant new way of addressing its audience when they're actually repeating something we know well already, using means which are completely familiar to us. Because very little is really new in the theatre – it's just the first time you yourself have seen it. I'm not very often overwhelmed by avant-garde work, or by much-praised directors riding on an international reputation. Too often, you see personal vanity at work rather than a strong desire to communicate. My best experiences have usually been in the relatively poor theatre – like my first sight of Robert Lepage doing wonderful things with the smallest of props.

ROBERT HEWISON:

Most West End productions.

JEREMY KINGSTON:

Plays in which someone is doing something that's been done already. People who are trying to be Ayckbourn, Pinter or Chekhov, and haven't skills. I don't think there's any subject I would say is a waste of time. But sometimes a very self-indulgent solo performance is a waste of time. From my point of view plays that show that God is good are a waste of time too.

ALASTAIR MACAULAY:

At one level – truly bad shows, like *Sunset Boulevard*, *Martin Guerre* – big flashy blockbusters. I don't enjoy seeing those – no civilized person could – but, since they are being presented in the name of art, then – yes, we should talk about them and say they are bad, (or good), and why. But oh! Having to sit through them! The other thing that is a total waste of time is the mediocre. It is a bore to go and see a moderately decent production of a moderately decent play, and it is hard work not to write a boring review of it.

SHERIDAN MORLEY:

Almost nothing. If you didn't believe that every night something wonderful might happen, you wouldn't go at all. Even if you have four or five bad nights, you will still go back on the sixth night waiting for the miracle. And it happens maybe twice or three times a year.

DAVID NATHAN:

Those plays that you come out of feeling only that you are two hours nearer your death. Those plays where everything has been predictable or silly. It's a pity that a lot of them do run for a very long time.

BENEDICT NIGHTINGALE:

I love the theatre and I seldom think I've completely wasted my time. I feel I have when I see second-rate copies of what's already of the second-hand. In other words – deadly theatre, as Peter Brook said. Then you do begin to feel a little bit sorry for yourself and you think, "Oh, maybe my job is not as great as I thought it was."

JOHN PETER:

Hardly anything is a waste of time because you can find something even in a bad play. It's actually quite useful to find out why bad is bad. But some really pedestrian production of a well-known work where you realize after the first half-hour that the director has nothing to say really is a waste of time. So are some really bad musicals.

IAN SHUTTLEWORTH:

A piece of theatre that doesn't seem to have a purpose, doesn't seem to exist for any reason – whether artistic or that intellectual. Something that's there just because the writer, director or whoever, wanted to have another line to put into his or her resume.

CHARLES SPENCER:

Very little. I quite like bad theatre. That's the good thing about reviewing. If you've got a terrible old play, it's quite fun to watch it because you know you'll have fun writing about it. I'm slightly suspicious of international productions. There's a great hype about the international directors. I suppose I'm essentially a parochial critic: I like stuff that's rooted in British culture. This is slightly mischievous but there's a school of thought among some of my colleagues that if it's foreign it must be good. Billington and Coveney tend to think like that. Lepage does pretty wonderful stuff, so does Peter Stein, but I hate it when people start regarding the theatre with reverence. I hate the guru aspect of it. I hate the idea of the theatre as some kind of a sacred art. Of course, it rises to that on some occasions but most of it is about entertainment or opening up people's eyes. Reverence is a very unhealthy attitude for a critic to have ... Of dislikes: I'm getting very bored by the mindless compilation musicals, of plundering the hits of the past. I'm getting slightly tired by what used to be called the new wave of comedians.

I find that in an average week, I see one thing which I like very much, two things which are interesting if not perfectly achieved, two which are bad. Which doesn't strike me as being a bad proportion.

JACK TINKER:

If you don't leave the theatre a little bit more aware of yourself, you have wasted your time. If I sat in a theatre for two and a half hours and either haven't laughed or been moved or fascinated as much as I would sitting at home watching half an hour of *Coronation Street*, then I wasted my time.

IRVING WARDLE:

Automatic routine Shakespeare revivals. I happen to be insensible to musicals, so that's usually a waste of time too. I just don't know what they're for. I don't know what the music is supposed to add.

MATT WOLF:

Something boring.

2

WHEN A REVIEW IS NOT A PAGE-TURNER

Playwrights:

Sir Alan Ayckbourn
David Edgar
Arnold Wesker

Directors:

Howard Davies
David Farr
Nicolas Kent
Sam Mendes
Katie Mitchell
Adrian Noble
Max Stafford-Clark

Producers:

Thelma Holt
Sir Cameron Mackintosh
Michael Morris
Tom Morris
Peter Wilkins

Press-Agents

Martin Coveney
Sharon Kean
Sue Rolfe
Joy Sapieka

They answer the question:

– When is reading a review a waste of time for you?

SIR ALAN AYCKBOURN:

When the review tells me nothing about the experience the critic has undergone. I'm interested in what they've perceived and what they've gained from seeing a show. Sometimes they seem to write about everything but the show. I don't care if they are a vegetarian and had trouble finding a restaurant before the performance. Or they missed their bus. I want to know how the play seemed to them. How it worked.

MARTIN COVENEY:

The ones that just retell the plot.

HOWARD DAVIES:

I very rarely learn anything more about the play from a review. Well, I'm in a slightly privileged position because I research the plays I work on.

DAVID EDGAR:

I can't think criticism could ever be a waste of time. You always learn something from it. At the end of the rehearsal process everybody is so worried about technical things, costumes and lighting, that they can't step backwards and take in the big picture. So the critics can suddenly remind you what the play is actually about, what its core is. They can also give you compliments you didn't look for. I can figure several in my case. One was by Harold Hobson, when he said that there was a play of mine with an ending as good as Agatha Christie's *Witness for the Prosecution*, which is wonderfully structured. Then a living critic compared me to Balzac, saying that Balzac wanted to be the secretary of his time and I had set out on the same mission.

DAVID FARR:

If a review is short, it can't pretend to properly engage with a piece of work. The amount of thought that a serious work of theatre requires takes months of preparation so that you can seriously respond to it on an intellectual creative level. To me if someone pretends to be responding in that way in 200 words – that's a waste of time. But if someone reacts very simply and instinctively to a piece of theatre saying, "I found this moving." – that to me is fine. That is not criticism though. That is just a particular person's reaction.

THELMA HOLT:

Never. As an actress I used to claim never to read reviews. A lot of us say that, and it is usually untrue. I have not acted since 1976, but I can still quote some of my own reviews – only the good ones, of course, as I have a selective memory! I have stored only one bad one because it was from Kenneth Tynan, and I adored him.

SHARON KEAN:

The ones that don't give an opinion.

NICOLAS KENT:

Most of the time reading criticism is a waste of time. I read reviews of my own work only insofar as I'm worried about what's happening in the box-office and whether people are buying tickets. There have been a few times when criticism has transcended advertisement. It's mainly been in the past. Kenneth Tynan managed to extend the repertoire of work being presented in Britain by drawing attention to particular European playwrights. Harold Hobson too, especially in regard to French drama. To some extent Michael Billington has influenced people to look at political drama.

SIR CAMERON MACKINTOSH:

When the critic is only interested in being clever and it's all about a quick sound-bite reaction and cheap jokes. Of course, a critic's job is also to be a journalist and he must be attractive for the reader, otherwise the editor will say, "We'll axe the drama criticism." But sometimes critics just get off on their own cleverness and then the review becomes nothing about the material they are reviewing. At that point I lose sympathy.

SAM MENDES:

When they merely retell the plot.

KATIE MITCHELL:

It's never a waste of time. It's always fascinating to read what people perceive of what you've done. And in many cases you learn how to improve your work, which is after all what we all want to do.

MICHAEL MORRIS:

When a review is badly written or when too many preconceptions have been brought to bear. An open mind is the most important thing for a critic. But it's rare.

TOM MORRIS:

Reading criticism is never a waste of time because I need to know what these people are writing.

ADRIAN NOBLE:

A wise theatre practitioner will actually read them all.

SUE ROLFE:

It's a waste of time reading lots of different reviews of the same people saying the same things. Or when you're convinced they are going to give a good review because they feel they ought to.

JOY SAPIEKA:

When I read reviews I always read the opening and closing paragraphs first, to get me an idea of how the review will go. The time I read a review extra carefully is when it is about a show I am working on and I am looking for quotes. I don't think reviews are a waste of time although I often disagree with them.

MAX STAFFORD-CLARK:

When it's a bad review of my production. I remember favorable reviews and I try not to remember less favorable ones.

ARNOLD WESKER:

I no longer read reviews.

PETER WILKINS:

When the criticism comes after the show has folded.

Part VII
Give-And-Take Time

1

I REGRET HAVING SAID . . . :
CRITICS OFFER THEIR APOLOGIES

Michael Billington
James Christopher
Michael Coveney
Nick Curtis
Nicholas de Jongh
Jane Edwards
John Elsom
Robert Gore-Langton
Bill Hagerty
Jeremy Kingston

Alastair Macaulay
Sheridan Morley
David Nathan
Benedict Nightingale
John Peter
Ian Shuttleworth
Charles Spencer
Jack Tinker
Irving Wardle
Matt Wolf

They answer the question:

– Do you have any regrets about anything which you've done or written as a critic?

MICHAEL BILLINGTON:

The one that hits me most is my notice of Pinter's play *Betrayal* which came out in the early '80s. I was incredibly dismissive, rude and abrupt about the play. I said it was no more than a high-class soap opera and that Pinter was betraying his talent. That comes back and haunts me because now I've studied the play, talked about it, rethought it, and I was totally wrong then. But would one want to rewrite what one wrote? In a way – no. It would be dishonest because I must have felt that at that time. As a critic you can't ever rewrite your past. What one would change is not the content of the reviews but the style sometimes. I'm much more haunted by badly expressed ideas or inelegant sentences or the wrong adjective than by the opinion itself.

JAMES CHRISTOPHER:

Yes, definitely. There's a couple of articles that make me shrivel. Sometimes in my younger days I was too keen to make a stance at the expense of the show to prove myself. It's easier to write a damning review and often more entertaining. But it can also be a little irresponsible.

MICHAEL COVENEY:

Sometimes, yes. But I don't think being right is the job actually. At the end of the day there's no right and no wrong. All that matters is what is interesting in what you wrote. I don't like critics who are so sure that they are right about everything. If you've done the best you can and you've done some kind of a job of conveying the experience – that's fine.

NICK CURTIS:

If I have any regrets it's that I tend to be too soft on a play rather than too hard. That for me is still the division between the London theatre critics: those who have up in their mind what the audience will think and those who tend to attempt to be generous or kind.

NICHOLAS DE JONGH:

I publicly retracted my review of David Hare's *Skylight*. I was so un-impressed by the play the first time I saw it and I was very moved by it the second time. I saw the light. I understood it. That's the only dramatic thing that happened in my critic's life. Once I have an opinion I tend not to regret it.

JANE EDWARDS:

Of course. Sometimes I've been able to put it right later but not always. One's bound to make mistakes.

JOHN ELSOM:

My only regrets have been when I've been rather weak or when I haven't said things as directly and straightforwardly as I should have.

ROBERT GORE-LANGTON:

A stack. I'm always getting things wrong and I've been rude about people. But any critic that doesn't have a million and one regrets probably isn't doing his job. I might have slagged off plays that had been works of a genius and I dare say if I'd been reviewing *Look Back in Anger*, I'd have probably thought that was crap.

BILL HAGERTY:

I tend to be too generous because I like theatre so much. Sometimes I just enthuse that something is good when perhaps it would be smarter to point out the deficiencies as well. And I've got things wrong. When I reviewed the musical *Fame*, I used the phrase *Fame sometimes is fleeting*. As it turned out, that was pretty dumb, because it's been running for three years already and the paper for which I reviewed it was closed down. I still think I was right: it's not a very good production. And the purpose is to give one's opinion. If you give your opinion honestly, no matter what that opinion is, then you can't really be wrong.

JEREMY KINGSTON:

I remember going completely up the wrong tree in the review of *Narrow Road to the Deep North* by Edward Bond. I also wrote a poor review of a production of *The Lower Depths* (Gorky) and I wish I hadn't. Then: I didn't like a production of a play translated by Ranjit Bolt, who used to work as a merchant banker and did his translating on the bus to work. I made a dismissive remark about being a merchant banker. I met him a couple of years later and he quoted this paragraph to me, which obviously had stuck in his head. A lot of water has gone under the bridge since then and he's a good friend now ... Generally my weakness is that I spend more time writing about the playwright than conveying the quality of the performance. Maybe this does relate to my entry into the theatre world as a writer rather than as a performer.

ALASTAIR MACAULAY:

Individual opinions in reviews I regret, insomuch as sometimes (not often) I change my mind. Often I feel I've done the best I can before my deadline, but not the best I should have done by the show. Didn't Valery say that a poem isn't finished, it's merely abandoned? Well, that's infinitely more true of reviews, especially those written for a newspaper. I can look at reviews I wrote ten years ago and start rewriting them.

SHERIDAN MORLEY:

You couldn't be a critic and not have regrets. We are not racing tipsters. They sometimes like to say, "Aha! He failed to recognize it!" Or the famous case: there was a show called *Charlie Girl* which ran for seven years and all that time they left my review outside the theatre. It said that the show deserved to last a night and it might last a week. They thought they were trying to remind critics how wrong they could be. But I was quite pleased because I still think I can write what I believe in and the public has an absolute right to prove us wrong. Some things you get right, others you get wrong. But that should not be the basis of the test. All you could do is to stay true to yourself. It's then rather interesting to see what the other critics believe in and even more interesting – to see what the theatre-goers believe in.

DAVID NATHAN:

More often than not I regret not the opinion I've expressed but the way I've expressed it.

BENEDICT NIGHTINGALE:

When I first started reviewing very long ago in Manchester, I was a bit like John Simon. But when you're young, you're a bit capricious, fling out opinions and you're very rude about people. Then, I didn't recognize David Hare's quality early enough. I'm always rather hard on him. He wrote me a letter saying, "Dear Benedict, why are you so nice to me in person and so horrible about my plays?" I'm very grateful I've never had to review the first production of either *The Birthday Party* or *Waiting for Godot*. I wonder if I would have passed that test. I don't think there's been a major test I feel I have to recant about.

JOHN PETER:

I have a few regrets. A long time ago I was very dismissive about a play called *AC/DC* because I didn't understand the title. If I had, I would have taken a very different line on the characters. I completely misunderstood the play and I still regret it. This was long before I became a full-time critic, so it probably wasn't very influential.

Once I wrote something about an actor and an actress in a play I didn't like. I didn't know that they had been living together, and what I wrote about the show sounded as if I'd been drawing a parallel between their personal relationship and their performance. I was very upset about it afterwards but there was nothing I could do.

Once or twice I fudged my opinions, though I don't think I was being dishonest, just indecisive.

IAN SHUTTLEWORTH:

I wish I were more voracious in seeing a broader range of theatre early on. I wish I had gone around deliberately amassing the experience which I now want to draw on. I still feel I'm catching up slightly. I wish I had started theatre criticism as a student, although student criticism is dreadfully sterile.

CHARLES SPENCER:

Oh, I've been wrong. Often. I was certainly wrong about Pinter's *Moonlight*. I said there was not much in it. I had a great blind spot about Pinter for years. I was wrong. As a young and very arrogant writer I wrote that Tom Stoppard was overrated. I can't believe how silly that was. I revere him now. No judgement should ever be cast in stone. I always say, "Never take theatre review that seriously. It's only one person's opinion and he might be wrong." My wife was a ballet dancer for many years. I've seen her crying over reviews of her work. I've always said, "I hope I've never made anyone cry."

JACK TINKER:

I've never regretted an opinion. I've always tried not to be rude about appearances, especially to women. But I was once with Elizabeth Taylor in *The Little Foxes*. It was a dreadful performance. I sneered at her and my quote got picked up by *The Los Angeles Times* and *The New York Times* and quoted everywhere. I really was ashamed afterwards. Because it was almost like saying she didn't know how to make a stage entry.

IRVING WARDLE:

I regret having joined the course of outrage against Edward Bond. Not that I've got very fond of Bond's work but I've sensed he knows his business very well. The things he has to say seem still compulsively ugly to me but I was certainly completely out of order when I dismissed his play *Saved*.

MATT WOLF:

I'd see shows again and if my opinion has changed, I'd write that. I've learned to do that. *The Herbal Bed* is a good example. Before, I thought it was embarrassing to admit to changing my mind. But theatre is a mutable art form – that's one of its glories.

2

IF I WERE YOU . . . : THEATRE-MAKERS OFFER THEIR ADVICE

Playwrights:

Steven Berkoff
David Edgar
Arnold Wesker

Directors:

Howard Davies
Sir Richard Eyre
Sir Peter Hall
Nicolas Kent
Katie Mitchell
Trevor Nunn
Max Stafford-Clark

Producers:

Thelma Holt
Sir Cameron Mackintosh
Michael Morris
Tom Morris
Peter Wilkins

Press-Agents

Sharon Kean
Sue Rolfe
Joy Sapieka

They answer the question:

– What is your advice to the critics?

STEVEN BERKOFF:

Wait rather than write immediately what they feel. The initial impression changes. To write immediately about something is very dangerous. They should let it mature, or see it again.

HOWARD DAVIES:

Get a proper life! It would also be nice to see in the newspaper two opinions. I'd welcome alternative reviewing styles every other day in the newspapers. The constant thing that theatre has done is to try and make the critics get more involved in the understanding of how it's made. Several years back at The National Theatre there was such a debate between the theatre practitioners and the critics – to get the critic to understand that they should engage much more with the world of theatre, rather than just see themselves as reporters. And it was a very unsuccessful day.

DAVID EDGAR:

First, it's good for the critics to know what the process is. Second, they should take advantage of the amount they see and write comparatively and analytically. Which some of them do.

SIR RICHARD EYRE:

Watch better!

SIR PETER HALL:

Don't do it for too long! I'm not against critics. But they are people as much susceptible to fashion as the rest of us. And it's a very difficult job to fill year after year after year.

THELMA HOLT:

My advice is simple: please remember when you go to the theatre that metaphorically everyone standing up there is wearing a tee-shirt declaring "I'm doing the best I can". There does not have to be a gentle kindness, but there must be some generosity of spirit. The critic also needs some humility.

SHARON KEAN:

Be accurate in the information. Never make factual errors because that's the only basis on which practitioners criticize a critic. They get so mad and then the poor critic has a terrible time. In a review about a play we did once, one of the critics said that the particular performer was miming badly his piano play. And he wasn't! He was a very good pianist in fact! Then the critic was upset and the actor, and the producer were upset.

NICOLAS KENT:

Go out and live a bit more. Take things in.

SIR CAMERON MACKINTOSH:

I don't think I have any advice to critics other than to stop being a critic when they get bored with the theatre. I'm sure they can give more advice to me. I just would like to see some new young critics come along to see the theatre through fresh eyes.

KATIE MITCHELL:

Direct something or act something. Experience the responsibility of making something. It would be fantastic if they could find a way which makes sense economically for them to see less work. It must be so hard for them to see so much! It would be lovely if they could be liberated from the overdose of a week of theatre.

MICHAEL MORRIS:

Never stop trying to understand the theatre process! Don't see the work in the theatre as just being a product, see it as a process. The show is never complete, it's always going to change.

TOM MORRIS:

I have no advice to critics such as they are. I do have advice to arts editors, which is: "Think about ways to reflect the most live branches of performance culture." I know some of them do. But I'm unwilling to impose a moral piece of advice on a form of journalism that has nothing to do with morality.

TREVOR NUNN:

I wouldn't dream of offering them advice. It's an honorable profession and although you hear from time to time anguished cries front dramatists, directors, and actors, saying to critics, "What have you ever created! What do you know of these processes?", I think on the whole it's undertaken honestly by the people who are a part of it.

SUE ROLFE:

Critics should take more in-depth look at the creative process. They should more often take themselves to the rehearsal room instead of sitting in their ivory towers. They are so often out of touch with new developments. They need to get in there and find out what's going on.

JOY SAPIEKA:

I would like them to free themselves, to come in with a totally open mind. Sometimes they can be surprised by the results. I prefer a critic who says honestly, "I came in here expecting a bad experience and I was surprised, and this and this is what changed my mind."

MAX STAFFORD-CLARK:

Everybody working in the theatre whether they are a critic, a director, or an actor has to be alert and responsive to new movements and new things.

ARNOLD WESKER:

Try to write plays, and drop your spites.

PETER WILKINS:

Critics will tell you they don't need to know the mechanics of putting on a play. Yet sometimes we feel on this side that if they did know it, they would be less harsh about what it is we have tried to achieve. Because we try to achieve it with little money and with an enormous amount of difficulties. I don't mean they have to be dishonest about what they say. But perhaps less cruelly judgmental. I do think that there is a change now: critics feel that if they criticize the commercial theatre too severely, they'll kill it.

Part VIII
Starring: The Critics
(16 Eye-Witness Stories About Critics
Related by Theatre-Makers
And Critics)

THE ULTIMATE SATISFACTION: A CRITIC LEADS THE AUDIENCE OUT OF A SHOW

Nick Curtis

During the Edinburgh Festival, I turned up for a show called *Stress Wars and How to Win Them*. There were about eight people in the audience. Not bad for Edinburgh actually. A man got up on stage and said that we were going to be seeing a fantastic show but all three actors had dropped out a week before it was due to go on. "So," he said, "the writer is going to perform it for you. He's in a cab somewhere in Edinburgh and will be here any minute." Myself and the entire audience sat there for 45 minutes waiting for the writer to turn up. Finally the man on the stage, who was the producer, ran out of things to say, so he turned all the lights up and started asking us what our jobs were and whether they were stressful. When he got to me I said, "I'm a theatre critic and I'm sorry but I don't believe this man is coming, so I'm going out." I left and the entire audience followed me out and demanded their money back.

That was the most useful piece of criticism I'd ever done. I'm quite proud of it and it epitomizes my attitude to theatre criticism. It reflects also the tolerance of the British audiences to the theatre. There is a tremendous forgiving attitude towards theatre here. Because a visit to the theatre takes much more effort and money than a visit to the cinema or hiring a video, people are automatically predisposed to enjoy it.

A CRITIC'S BLESSING IN DISGUISE

Peter Hall

When I was starting the RSC, we were coming with the company in London and opening a theatre here for the first time. Throughout the season before that, Harold Hobson of *The Sunday Times* thought it was a very bad idea that we were going to do modern plays as well as Shakespeare and that we were coming to London. In every review about our Stratford productions that year, he said that this was good or this was bad but he certainly hoped he was not going to see it in London. When he had done this about six times, I wrote to the editor, "Mr. Hobson is absolutely entitled to his opinion that the RSC shouldn't be coming to London, but he has made his prejudice clear and I can't afford to have him say that in every article for every play. Would you please send your second critic from now on to our plays." There was a Pandemonium: "The public has a right to know!" "You can't dictate to newspaper!" Etc. But it ended with Hobson taking me out to lunch and saying that he was only being mischievous and trying to get the debate going, and that he wished me luck in founding the RSC.

CRITICS DISMISSED

Ian Herbert

I was once in Leningrad, as it then was, at a meeting of critics. There was a very formal sit-down reception and I found myself next to the great director Tovstonogov. Desperately trying to think of something to say, I made the mistake of asking him what he thought of theatre critics. "Theatre critics do three things, which as director I do not find useful. First, they tell me what the play is about – this I already know. Then they tell me how they would direct the play – this I do not need to know. Then they tell me if they like the play – this I do not want to know." I was too embarrassed to take the conversation any further, but I thought to myself how right he was. The critic isn't a would-be director, he's an informed member of the audience. It's from the actors and the director that the wonder of theatre experience comes, and where the creativity lies. All we as critics can do is try to say, "Wow!" in as intelligent and entertaining a way as possible.

TURMOIL IN THE CRITICS' BRETHEN

Nick Hern

I asked Michael Coveney if he would keep a diary of a year in the life of a theatre critic. He thought that was fun and we then produced a sort of a facetious book. The aim was to recount what happened in a critic's life other than the criticism. In passing he had a little run-down of the qualities of his fellow-critics, including description of their sartorial habits – what shoes they wear, how large they are, etc. In much the same spirit Coveney said that Milton Shulman had managed to fail to notice the talents of ... and there was a list of writers. The book was published in April. It wasn't till August that it came to Shulman's attention. I then got a phone-call from him followed by a seven-page letter full of the original cuttings from *The Evening Standard*, now yellowing with age, to prove that he had indeed spotted talent in this or the other writer. We tried to tell him that Michael wasn't serious and the book was not meant in earnest, but Shulman was in earnest and he threatened to sue. His lawyer, a very respected one, said he had a case. We could have either gone to court, which would have cost thousands of pounds, or we could settle. So we settled. We paid him some money, we paid his lawyer's costs, and had to take an advertisement in *The Observer* and in one of the trade journals saying that Michael Coveney and the publisher apologize.

FAMILY TIES WITH A CRITIC? GOD FORBID!

Thelma Holt

The only really ghastly review I have had for my productions as opposed to when I was acting, was for *Electra* directed by Deborah Warner with Fiona Shaw in the title role. I was not angry because of this review, but the lack of knowledge of the piece and understanding of what we were trying to do caused me some embarrassment, as it had been written by my niece-by-marriage. I was able to walk into the dressing-room where there were some very bruised egos and say the piece was not just about the show, it was her "let's kick auntie moment." I excused her on the grounds that she was trying very hard not to be partisan.

A STUNNING ACHIEVEMENT: A 20-MINUTE PLAY PUTS A CRITIC TO SLEEP

Nicolas Kent

A funny story with a critic involved is a contradiction of terms! Interestingly there is a major English critic who comes here, to the Tricycle, and seems incapable of getting the plot of any show right. In his reviews of two of our shows he got the plot completely wrong. Recently we did a very straightforward 20-minute play with a beginning, a middle and an end and, and he managed to misinterpret the plot. I thought that was a stunning achievement! I think he went to sleep. But how can a critic sleep during a 20-minute play?

TESTING THE PATIENCE OF A CRITIC

Sir Cameron Mackintosh

It was the first night of *Trelawney*, the very first musical which I ever brought to London at the age of 26. The First Night was a 7-o'clock curtain. The great critic, Harold Hobson, was still alive and writing for *The Sunday Times*, and a review by him could make the world turn – he was so powerful. Harold being slightly crippled liked to get to the theatre early because he didn't like people seeing him limp down the aisle. I arrived slightly shaken in the foyer of Sadler's Wells theatre having just wished everyone good luck backstage where Max Adrian (in his last stage appearance) said to me "Thank you, dear boy, I'll be giving my notice tomorrow as three of my lines have been cut!", to find Harold Hobson having a terrible row with the Front of House Manager as his two usual front row seats had been removed to make way for a false proscenium for the show. He was preparing to leave as he didn't want to sit in alternative seats and enter the by now nearly full auditorium. I begged him to review the show, pleading it was my West End debut and my career was in the balance. He relented and went in. By now in desperate need of a drink, I was anxiously waiting for the show to start. 7.00 p.m. came and went, the foyers were empty but the show still hadn't commenced. I went backstage at ten past seven and found the Company Manager who, ashen faced, told me the orchestra hadn't been called till the normal performance time of 7.30. By now the audience was getting restless. At 7.15 there were only 4 musicians out of 18. At about 7.20 I just had to start with what we had. Luckily it was a very long opening number called "Pull Yourself Together", which was very appropriate at the time. During the opening number the other dozen musicians arrived, so by the end of the number I had a full orchestra. Still it was most terrifying night in my life. Luckily Harold liked the show.

A ONE-LINE REVIEW

Sheridan Morley

I was at the first night of Peter O'Toole's *Macbeth*, which was never as bad as most of us critics actually said. It was actually worse. Coming out of the theatre two men were leaving before me. One of them turned to his friend and said, "Well, all I hope now is that the dog has not been sick in the car". I thought that was the best review of that production I'd ever heard. I love stories of the audience because they are very often better reviewers than we are.

A CRITIC STEALS THE SHOW (I)

Sam Mendes

It was on the first night of *Cabaret*. In the interval Alan Cumming, who played the MC, was under instructions from me to go in to the audience and dance with somebody. He danced with a critic. There were fantastic expressions on the other critics' faces! They went from horror that they might be chosen to absolute hysteria. I thought that was a sort of unifying moment. Critics were definitely part of that audience, they couldn't stand outside that experience. They were terrified that they would be picked, and they were howling with laughter when one of their kind was chosen. I remember Michael Coveney in *The Observer*: "At last it's happened! Someone has danced with a critic on an opening night." That was fun.

A CRITIC STEALS THE SHOW (II)

Ian Shuttleworth

In 1995, in Edinburgh, there was a performer called Graham Fellows who had created a character called John Shuttleworth – a no-hope amateur, 50-year-old singer and song-writer of boring cliché songs. A couple of audience members walked to the box-office and asked for tickets for the Ian Shuttleworth show ... It flattered my ego for a while. And life is now imitating art: in 1997, I'm performing a show of my own, about being a critic, at the same venue.

KISS OF THE UNKNOWN WOMAN

David Nathan

Once at the Dirty Duck after a Stratford first night with Michael Coveney and Pam Harris, half-way through the meal a woman came up to me and said, "David Nathan?" I said, "Yes." "I heard you were in the pub. So I had to come up and say hello," she said and kissed me on both cheeks. "Who's that?" asked Michael. I said, "I don't know!" Pam said, "Oh, that's Jan Chapelle. She is a witch in *Lady Macbeth*." About an hour later I saw Jan in the corner and said, "Jan, forgive me, I've been trying for an hour to remember where we've met and I can't." "We've never met," she said, "21 years ago I was in a Snoo Wilson play at the Bush theatre and you gave me such a wonderful notice that I was encouraged to go on." And she quoted some of the notice. I got back home and looked it up in my files. She had quoted it correctly and she must have been about 16 at the time! That was a marvelous thrill. It meant that I'd done my job and discovered or at least encouraged some new talent.

THE ENLIGHTENMENT OF A CRITIC

Trevor Nunn

Michael Billington is a critic that I greatly respect. When I originally took over as the artistic director of the RSC, I employed him to edit the magazine *Fanfare*. Therefore we have always had a very good working and conversational relationship. So when at the RSC my colleague John Caird and I did an adaptation of the Dickens' novel *Nicholas Nickleby*, I was really deeply shocked to discover that Michael Billington not only said that he had no sympathy with the endeavor, but he said he felt that it was a project that should never have existed. It was, he said, the responsibility of a subsidized company, such as the RSC, to do a wealth of existing dramatic material from all the different strands of European culture, to find the neglected works in the English language, and not to create new ones through the process of adaptation. The production itself was not the point. It had a generally bad critical reaction which was altogether vanquished by the public reaction. The critics were present when the entire audience stood at the interval and again as the cast reassembled for part II, and the audience was weeping and cheering, and going down the isles to the front of the stage minutes before the show had actually finished. But the critics didn't write about that. They denied the existence of that and discussed the production in rather dry and academic terms. I was particularly disappointed that Michael Billington took that attitude. And he not only took it once, he took it again and again, because the production was so popular that it was revived on five separate occasions. Every time he wrote the same extreme rejection of the nature of the piece. At the time *The Guardian* ran a "highly recommended" section and although by then *Nicholas Nickleby* had achieved a legendary status, the title never once appeared in this column. It was as if the readership of that paper were being told, "This is not for you." The last time that it was revived, I had just made a film and Michael Billington phoned me and said, "I've been asked to do an interview with you about the film and the only time I can do it is in the morning of the first performance of that latest version of *Nicholas Nickleby*." I said, "Michael, surely you're not going to review it again." "Of course, I am!", he said. "But you've written exactly the same thing four times! Give somebody else the chance to write about it." He said, "There's always a possibility that I would think differently and I think it's my responsibility to come and see it." We had our meeting about the film and it was a pleasant talk, and at the end I said, "I mustn't keep you from your appointment. You must sharpen your carving knives and work out how you can write vitriolically about *Nicholas Nickleby* again. But I'll tell you one thing: you've said all this time that the show doesn't really have the right to exist because it's not a play. This most recent revival has come two years after all the other revivals, and the work is now published. Consequently instead of reviving something that lives in everybody's memory as an on-going piece of work in the company's repertoire, I've come to it as a text. And I've discovered that it's the most thrillingly coherent play by David Edgar about money. I don't know any more acute, far-reaching or scathing examination of the lure, power and corruption of money in all our lives." On the following Monday morning his *Guardian* review began, "*Nicholas Nickleby* is the best play about money that has been written in English language in this century". So he did finally recant, which I admired him for. However I don't think it would have happened had it not been for that somewhat collusive conversation. It was interesting that by then it was possible for him to say, "I should have recognized that it was a play, and not as it was – a shapeless adaptation".

THE REVENGE OF THE PR

Sue Rolfe

There was a particular journalist assigned to review a show I was publicizing. He decided to be extremely clever and made loud remarks sitting in the third row from the front. Of course, I had all the numbers of the seats, so I knew where everybody was sitting. By the interval the producer was running around looking for me and asking who that man was. His behaviour was reported to the editor of the paper and, I'm afraid, he was fired.

THE PERILS OF OVERNIGHT REVIEWING

Jack Tinker

Once I had to review *The Little Foxes*. I ran out of the theatre, jumped in a taxi and wrote the review on my way home. Then I jumped out of the taxi, paid the driver and when it went away, I realized I had left my keys in it. I was locked out of my flat. So I thought, "My God! Who's the most boring person in this block of flats who is bound to be in at 10:30 in the evening?" I pressed the flat N25. "Yes?" "I've got to use your phone!" I rushed up. As I went into the sitting room I did notice that my neighbour was standing up with a towel around himself but I thought he had just had a bath or a shower and was going to bed. I got on the phone and I read the review through. When I finished it, I realized that right in front of me there was a totally naked blonde. She said, "So you didn't enjoy the play?" She had been sitting there and I hadn't noticed at all. So that is how the 10:30 dead-line concentrates your mind.

ART VERSUS MONEY

Steven Berkoff

One day, at the Almeida theatre, there was a meeting to discuss the theatre. There was the director of the Royal Court and some other characters were there, and Michael Billington. All they talked about was funding: whether there should be greater funding for the arts or less funding; whether they should get more, as Germany gets more ... In the end I said, "Why don't you just talk about art for once? About content!" The whole audience clapped!

SOMETIMES MONEY DOES MATTER
or
IGNORANCE REVEALED

Peter Wilkins

At a luncheon party I was sitting next to a critic. It was at the time when we had produced a play by Eugene O'Neill, which had been written in 1929 and was originally produced in two nights. We did it in one night starting at 6 o'clock in the evening until 11 o'clock. I said to him, "Yes, we are proud to have done it. But we lost £83,000." Which in those days was quite a bit of money. He said, "Well, money isn't everything." I thought, "What does this man think we are actually doing? We are in the commercial theatre. We're putting on plays to make money. We've lost a certain sum of money and he's dismissing it as if there's no consequence! This man doesn't understand what the commercial business is about!" That same critic was slightly critical over the fact that we had put on another play, at the Haymarket theatre, which was very successful and had paid for the £83,000 we had lost on the other play. Yet he dismissed it as being a pot-boiler and a trivial rubbish. Well, we were doing the "trivial rubbish" in order to pay for the thing that he thought we should be proud of. That's a bit worrying when a major critic on a major newspaper doesn't quite appreciate what it is you are trying to do.

EPILOGUE:
FOR AND AGAINST LONDON THEATRE CRITICISM:
A FOREIGNER'S VIEW

So? Did I finally discover my ideal for theatre criticism in London? The answer is "Yes" and "No". If not the ideal, though, I did discover a very worthy and admirable model of theatre criticism – an exemplar of the golden middle way. Not a star who calls the shots, as is the case in New York. Neither a lofty scholar nor a biased insider, as is mostly the case in Eastern Europe. But a passionate, knowledgeable and very strict keeper of the score of the theatre. That's what London theatre criticism is. When it's at its very best, of course.

AN EULOGY FOR LONDON THEATRE CRITICISM

It's well known that British theatre critics are at their strongest when they describe what's happening on the stage. What I find even more admirable is their ability to transform their emotions into indisputable facts – to make emotion seem pragmatic, to subdue it within an ostensibly unbiased reportage. Everything they describe appears so plausible and convincing that you forget that it's only one person's perception and you kind of take it as an account of the objective truth. This extraordinary skill makes every exemplary review in London sound like a par excellence lawyer's plea. The difference is that while lawyers turn facts into heartbreaking emotion, London critics turn heartbreaking emotion into convincing facts. The approaches may be different but the result is similar: an emotional interpretation of a certain reality meant to move and persuade the judges, the judges being the readers in the latter case.

However, unlike their New York counterparts, London theatre critics are not star lawyers. Not that they wouldn't like to aspire to a star status but they are a priori spared that temptation. Because, whereas in New York theatre criticism itself is a spectacle, sometimes even more interesting than its object – the theatre, in Britain the unsurpassable spectacle is the theatre itself. So London critics have to put up with the fact that they will never play the lead and will always be cast in the more inconspicuous role of ordinary, though skillful, lawyers of a star client. But they are lawyers of such a kind without whom the theatre wouldn't be as brilliant a star as it is. Because while keeping its score, they are also maintaining its standards.

Actually, in regard to its nature the role of the London critics very much resembles that of the Chorus in the ancient Greek drama. It's neither a leading nor a supporting role. At one and the same time it's part of the theatre and its independent commentator. It's like a huge screen put above the stage to show the audience the close-ups of what's happening on the stage. It's like a portion of the audience allowed onto the stage. Finally, it's like an echo of the theatre, which comes back to it, so that it could hear its voice the way the audience hears it.

In other words, London theatre critics play a predominantly formative role in the long-term destiny of London theatre. And this is one of the substantial differences between New York and London theatre criticism: whereas the New York critics' role is very influential in the short-run of New York theatre life, London critics are cast in a very influential role in the long-run of London theatre life.

What makes London theatre critics qualify as standard-keepers of their theatre is that they are enthusiasts of the theatre in principle, not of separate theatre events. As a springboard for their writing they use a philosophy for the theatre – what it should be – and a desire to bridge the gap between this ideal and reality. They seek every occasion – a show, a play, a topic, acting or directing style – to draw general conclusions about the development of the British theatre, its traditions and new tendencies, its virtues and vices.

This state-of-the-theatre approach of London theatre critics can most easily be observed in the long articles and reviews in the Sunday papers. But there is a whiff of it in the short daily reviews of all major London critics as well, especially when read on a regular basis. The state-of-the-theatre core of the London theatre criticism, I think, is the key to the delicate balance of information, wisdom and concern, typical for every exemplary theatre review and article there – a balance which, for me, is the trademark of the London theatre criticism, rather than its renowned irony.

The concern London theatre critics feel and express towards their theatre is of a special nature. It's a concern of insiders and outsiders at one and the same time. And this is another manifestation of the golden-middle-way attitude adopted by the London critics. Because they are a part of the theatre community just as much as they are a part of the journalistic community. With an amazing ease they stride the tiny strip where these two worlds meet and very rarely do they lose their balance. I'm very impressed by and highly appreciative of their ability to fraternize with theatre-makers, act sometimes as theatre practitioners, sit on financial bodies' panels and attend cocktail parties thrown by the theatres in their honour, and then make no bones about saying exactly what they think about the very same people they've been mixing with.

The fact that London critics do not consider theater liaisons dangerous is, I think, derivative of the special kind of neutrality they maintain towards the theatre. It's not the almost objective neutrality of their New York colleagues, who try to keep their hands clean by staying entirely apart from the theatre. It's more of an innate neutrality. I'd call it a neutrality of the inner freedom, that is they are so innately free as a disposition towards life, and respectively towards the theatre, that they consider it a matter-of-course to both socialize with theatre-makers and openly criticize them. People who are not so innately free usually call such a behaviour courageous because they associate it with the agony of overcoming biases, scruples and partialities. But for those who have developed this type of inner freedom, the neutrality derivative from it is as normal as breathing and does not cost them special efforts or soul torments.

London theatre critics are well aware of the significant role they play in regard to the financial fortune of the theatre. And they do write articles which help theatre institutions and artists get funding (for example, The Theatre Museum). But very seldom are they supportive just for the sake of it. Because they are also aware of the indisputable fact that compromises in the short run actually only endorse low standards in the long run. Being supportive at the expense of their critical standards is marked as a sin deep down in their moral code, exactly because of the dual nature of their concern for the theatre – the theatre they are fighting for and criticizing at one and the same time. Not by chance one of the main controversies in the New York theatre community – the issue of constructive and destructive criticism – is not remotely an apple of discord in the London theatre community.

London theatre critics are a living embodiment of the ideal of the American theatre-makers, and probably of theatre-makers from everywhere, in one more aspect: that they always place the theatre piece they review in the context of the whole body of work of its creators. Whereas New York critics are usually blamed for reviewing each and every show as a phenomenon entirely separated from the rest of the work of its creators. The diametrically different approaches of the critics in New York and London in this respect reflect the different attitudes of British and Americans toward success. To be successful is not only the No. 1 goal in America; success there is always only in the present tense. Lying on old laurels does not bring any dividends in regard to the present statute of American artists. In Britain, in the first place, success is not everything, and, secondly, both life and art there is viewed as an incessant process in which failure and success are connected and interrelated. Which is why theatre critics there are like family doctors of the London stages: always aware of the current shape and the previous condition of their patient – year after year and every single day. Therefore their diagnosis of their theatre is likely to be more accurate than the one the New York theatre gets from the New York critics, who judge it most often on a day-to-day, show-by-show basis. However, the London theatre critics' approach in this respect could also go to an extreme. And it does, when, for example, critics refer to a show they have seen so long ago that hardly anybody remembers – something of which some people in the London theatre community complain.

"Community" is a word which perfectly fits London theatre critics' society. Being together almost every evening to see a first night in London or outside of it makes critics there even look like a big and well-knit family, every member of which is very familiar with the habits of the rest. And this is not only on the surface. There is a real sense of community among London theatre critics despite the inevitable likes and dislikes. In my interviews with them, very rarely did they utter a word against each other. On the contrary, they talked with admiration about their colleagues. This is something which very much differentiates them from the New York critics, most of whom hardly missed a chance, in my interviews with them, to point out that so-and-so was an idiot and that I shouldn't even bother to talk with so-and-so because it would be a waste of time. At the end of my work on my New-York critics book, when my interviewees were approving the final texts, they crossed out all the vilifications: frankly, the cut material was enough to form a separate chapter. The fact that I didn't have the same experience in London might well have been a manifestation of the theatricality of British life in principle. However, I believe, that this was not only a result of the famous British courtesy (a stiff-upper-lip attitude towards the negative qualities of colleagues?) but also, and more so, a question of a general attitude towards life, friends and professional relationships.

It's really striking how very down-to-earth London theatre critics are! For example, I can hardly imagine most of the leading New York critics riding the subway or going back home after the show on a late bus. Such a thing is a matter-of-course for London theatre critics. Just as it is a matter-of-course for them to travel all the time to visit theatres outside London. The unceasing year-round activity of the British theatre, which requires their presence almost five nights a week, has made them tough, hard-working men and women who look like supermen/women compared to their rather spoiled New York colleagues.

Down-to-earth, too, is their criticism. Very knowledgeable, but never dryly theoretical or loftily speculative, it's full of comparisons and references to current events, people, tendencies, always trying to place the show under review in the context of contemporary life. Technical effects and spectacular sets do not very much impress London theatre critics. What matters for them is life on stage and whether it says something to people sitting in the theatre. That's why they are better at describing human characters and relations rather than the interiors in which these relations take place.

In short, London theatre criticism is an advocacy of life. While New York critics tend to overpraise and overblame the shows they review, London critics are more apt to not go to extremes, the same way as life rarely go to extremes. Metaphorically speaking, New York criticism is like somebody elbowing one's way to make an impression on the readers and then fighting to keep their attention by all means. Whereas London criticism is like a much more modest person, with much less glamor to offer, but with no need for it because the communication with their readers is a priori on a more substantial and in-depth level.

The difference between New York and London criticism in this respect is a very accurate reflection of the main differences of the two cultures in their attitudes towards reality. On the one hand, there is the American obssession with success by all means, and the derivative hit-flop mentality and need for putting luster on reality (because imperfect is only the reality of failure!). On the other hand, there is the very pragmatic, down-to-earth, British approach to life, taking it with all its beautiful and ugly faces. Therefore New York criticism may seem more theatrical on the whole, but it's actually a little bit overinflated. Whereas London criticism is more truthful to reality, reflecting both theatre and life as they are. In this respect, New York criticism resembles a colour broad-screen movie, while London criticism is more like an Italian neo-realism movie.

The palpable fleshiness of London criticism brings out one more comparison. Theatre criticism in principle is a very impressionistic art form: it has to "catch the moment" and freeze it on a page, it has to make theatre seem three-dimensional on a two-dimensional piece of paper. When a critic has the talent to do so, he/she is the only person in the very transient and ephemeral art of theatre who can make the time stop. However, New York and London theatre criticism are impressionistic in a very different way. New York criticism is more like a painting of Claude Monet – ephemeral like a mirage, carefree, spared the burden of flat colours. Whereas London theatre criticism is more like a painting of Edward Manet – a mixture of impressionism and realism: more luscious and sultry, delving deeper into the human dramas. "At its best British criticism does much the same as British acting does, which is psychological truth to the moment," says the British critic Paul Allen. In my opinion, this is the best encapsulation of the kind of impressionism the equivalent of which London theatre criticism is: not only visually truthful to the moment but psychologically deep as well, i.e. recreating both human behaviour and human dramas in a thrilling three-dimensional way.

The sense of humour of London theatre critics is also very humane. It's not destructive, as it frequently is in the critiques of their New York counterparts. Humour in London theatre criticism is rather the humour of paradox and of colourful puns, the Buster Keaton style of humour which doesn't destroy but just makes fun of people's shortcomings and misbehaviour. On the whole London theatre critics are more tolerant in their criticism. They don't have the hit-or-miss mentality of their New York colleagues. They are more willing to let artists fail because theatre is just a continuation of life and failure is just as natural as success.

EVERY SILVER LINING HAS ITS CLOUD

Failure is not something London theatre critics themselves are spared. They have their good and bad days like everybody else. On bad days, they miss the points and the plots of the shows, they drop their pads after their heads droop in an irresistible doze in the dark of the theatres, or they simply write dull and faceless reviews.

Paradoxically, what makes London theatre criticism less of an ideal is precisely the things that make it close to the ideal. First of all, it's the very theatre situation in London. The constant inflow of theatre, brilliant or not, is a double-edged weapon for criticism. On the one hand, it's a real blessing for critics, and has certainly made them the best specialists in their field in the whole world, if only for the mere fact of having seen so much theatre. On the other hand, this all-year-round theatre can turn the critics' profession into a conveyer-belt job, deprived of the inspiration and freshness of the extraordinary. Probably it's exactly for this reason that most of London theatre critics refer to their profession as a *job* not as a *vocation*, whereas their American colleagues rarely miss a chance to passionately point out that it's criticism they've been born to do. In London, first-class premieres follow one another at such a pace that there's no time for the very special thrill of the expectation. In this respect, London theatre critics are like spoiled children with so many wonderful and expensive toys that they have lost the ability to yearn for another one and skip about it when they get it.

The overdose of theatre exposes London critics to one more risk, the risk of losing their firm bond with life outside the stage. After a certain point, not life but theatre becomes your reality and your reference point as well, which could automatically suffocate and distort critics' criteria. Because one could start comparing things from the theatre primarily with other things from the theatre. I myself experienced this when I entered the London theatre marathon. After 14 shows in my first 10 days there, I had the feeling that I was living in a surreal world. Having entered this surreal world, one could start writing mainly for people with a similar experience and knowledge of the theatre. Which in the end could inconspicuously deprive critics of their main mission – to convert people to the religion of theatre.

Instead, they could start talking only to the already ordained. And for the readers it's not that important how this, say, 18th *Hamlet* stands compared to the other 17 a critic has seen. What's important is how it stands compared to reality: how it smells, tastes, and feels like. And all this is best described with smells, tastes and feelings not from the theatre but from life.

It really seems a miracle to me how London theatre critics manage to escape the risk of these traps most of the time. Maybe their renowned pragmatism is their very reliable safeguard.

There is one point, though, in which even this safeguard often betrays them. And it's when it comes to judging new plays. The example to the whole theatre world of sustained concern for nurturing young playwrights in Britain is another double-edged weapon. In their desire to encourage new drama, London critics all of a sudden turn into parents enchanted by almost everything their children do. It's amazing to me how easily they pile praise upon praise over the fledgling playwrights and their often quite minor achievements. In this, they resemble the "Thumbs Up!" and "Thumbs Down!" approach of their American colleagues from the TV stations and tabloid papers, only that they definitely prefer the "Thumbs Up!" type of review. In the end, this initially noble tendency of London critics turns into a bad service for young playwrights. Because debutantes become intoxicated by success, and it is a universal truth that swollen heads are rarely visited by the muses again. Then, this also becomes a time-bomb placed by the critics themselves under the future standards of the theatre.

The extreme benevolence of the critics towards the new drama of the past few years is not only a result of a noble concern for the theatre. It's also underpinned by some kind of fear of not missing the next genius and of being ridiculed for this by posterity. This fear is entirely inexplicable to me, because most of the critics themselves point out that criticism is not a question of being right or wrong. Also, because it's exactly Kenneth Tynan who has been proven wrong in some major cases and yet his criticism has outlived that of those now seen to be correct.

Kenneth Tynan is at the bottom of another problem for London theatre criticism. I would call it the Kenneth Tynan's shadow problem, that is the subconsciously preconceived awareness by critics of the impossibility of ever surpassing his talent for fiery, brilliant prose. It is as if, from the start of their careers, they know that they enter a competition with a foregone conclusion. Having a priori given up the idea of ever beating his literary-critical record, most of them establish an idolatrous relationship with Kenneth Tynan, therefore ordaining one of the very few idols of the otherwise cult-free English stage. The other consequence is that critics have become more concerned with *what* they say than with *how* they say it. This, added to the generally subjugated emotion, makes their criticism sometimes rather even and not always very impressive as prose writing.

Another problem of London theatre criticism, which has nothing to do with critics themselves, is the very little time criticism gets on TV. It's astonishing that, in a country where theatre is of such importance, the major TV channels not only do not have their own on-staff critics, but they do not have many, if any, shows devoted to the theatre on a regular basis!

Whatever the external problems and the internal shortcomings of London theatre criticism, the list of its virtues and advantages is far more extensive, important and impressive. And while New York critics are to be envied for the extremely significant role they play in the current life of New York theatre as a make-or-break corrective, London critics are to be envied for two far better reasons: the theatre itself they have the chance to be criticizing; and their ability to serve it humbly while actually shaping its future in the long run.

INDEX

Other titles in the Contemporary Theatre Studies series:

Other titles in the Contemporary Theatre Studies series:

This book is part of a series. The publisher will accept continuation orders which may be cancelled at any time and which provide for automatic billing and shipping of each title in the series upon publication. Please write for details.